NO RIVER TO CROSS

NO RIVER TO CROSS

TRUSTING THE ENLIGHTENMENT THAT'S ALWAYS RIGHT HERE

DAEHAENG SUNIM

FOREWORD BY ROBERT BUSWELL

Wisdom Publications • Boston

Wisdom Publications
199 Elm Street
Somerville MA 02144 USA
www.wisdompubs.org

Library of Congress Cataloging-in-Publication Data
Daehaeng, Sunim.
  No river to cross : trusting the enlightenment that's always right here / Dae-
haeng Sunim.
    p. cm.
  Includes bibliographical references.
  ISBN 0-86171-534-9 (pbk. : alk. paper)
  1. Spiritual life—Zen Buddhism. 2. Women Buddhist priests—Korea (South) I.
Title.
  BQ9288.T35 2007
  294.3'444—dc22

                                 2007021084

ISBN 0-86171-488-1

11 10 09 08
 5 4 3 2

Cover design by Rick Snizik. Interior design by Tony Lulek. Set in Weiss 11/15.

CONTENTS

FOREWORD

The contributions ordained women traditionally have made to Korean Buddhism, and continue to make today, have been unconscionably neglected. Korean Buddhist monastic records offer little information on the activities of women. There is some evidence about nuns during the Silla dynasty (57 B.C.E.–935 C.E.), a bit more about Buddhist women in general during the golden age of Buddhism during the Goryeo dynasty (935–1392), but again next to nothing during the Joseon period (1392–1910), when women suffered under an oppressive social system and Buddhism endured the persecution of Confucian ideologues. Despite this apparent invisibility of nuns, Korean Buddhist nuns have actually made tremendous strides in bettering themselves and their tradition over the last quarter of the twentieth century. And among the current generation of eminent nuns, no one's star shines more brightly than does that of Daehaeng Kun Sunim; indeed, there is no other nun who has been more influential in both the Jogye Order and Korean society at large.

In contemporary Korean Buddhism, Daehaeng Kun Sunim is one of the most renowned and respected figures and certainly one of the most influential nuns ever to have been active in the tradition. Daehaeng Kun Sunim has impeccable credentials as a *seon* master, having spent long years of training deep in the mountains of Korea before she began to teach. She is widely recognized in Korea as a teacher of profound insight and compassion, who has guided thousands of nuns, monks, and laypeople throughout her career. Her disciples, quite unusually, also include a number of monks—something unheard of previously in a monastic tradition where nuns are subordinate to monks. The organization she founded over three decades ago, the Hanmaum Seonwon, has emerged as one of the most influential Korean Buddhist institutions today, with over fifteen domestic branches and ten overseas centers.

Daehaeng Kun Sunim's ability to reach out to a wide audience of both ordained and lay Buddhists is well documented in this anthology *No River to Cross*. Her method of teaching is disarmingly simple, yet remarkably profound. She is widely known for her insight into people's character and her ability to draw on that insight to craft teachings that correspond precisely to the needs of her audience. Arranged like traditional Indian Sutra, *No River to Cross* organizes Daehaeng Kun Sunim's teachings in a way that is readily accessible to scholars and students alike. Daehaeng Kun Sunim emerges in this collection as one of the most creative and accessible of contemporary Korean Buddhist teachers, capable of using even the most mundane of daily events as grist for the mill of Buddhist teaching and practice.

Robert Buswell, Director of the Center for
Buddhist Studies, UCLA

How to get people to wake up from the dream—this is the problem faced by awakened ones since time immemorial. Having tasted freedom for themselves, they are loath to leave others behind, knowing "I too suffered like that, I too behaved like that when I was ignorant and didn't know any better." Seeing the damage caused by not understanding that everything is part of themselves, that everything shares the same life and mind, those who have awakened point straight at the moon: "Do you see?" Trying to entice children out of a burning house, they communicate through both words and our fundamental mind.

Sometimes people only stare at the teacher's finger; sometimes they run back into the house, saying that it's warmer inside. Sometimes awakened masters cry tears of unbounded heartache; sometimes they cry tears of deep joy. Whether they're revered or reviled matters not a bit to them. They live not for the pleasures of the body, nor merely out of habit. Rather, they live to see people become just a little wiser than they were before, to see people open their eyes to the infinite ability within, where concepts and thoughts of "I" are incinerated like dry weeds in a furnace.

Daehaeng Kun Sunim is such a person. With compassion and deep insight, she teaches everyone who wants to listen.

She teaches the path to awakening in direct terms, so that anyone, regardless of circumstance, can practice and awaken. For ultimately it is not our circumstances that hinder us—it is our own thoughts. Through our likes and dislikes, our blame and resentment, we end up living in a self-created fog, not knowing where to turn or how to live. Daehaeng Kun Sunim shows us not only how to dissolve this fog, she also shows us the liberating power of our inherent nature.

However, Daehaeng Kun Sunim can only point the way. It's up to you to put your understanding into practice. Discover the treasure that transcends all words and claim your inheritance as a human being.

Chong go Sunim

A BRIEF BIOGRAPHY OF
DAEHAENG KUN SUNIM

Daehaeng *Kun Sunim*[1] was born in 1927 to an aristocratic family. The family's status ensured that they were originally quite wealthy, but by the time of Sunim's birth their situation was precarious; Imperial Japan's efforts to colonize Korea led to a military occupation of Korea that began in 1904 and became progressively more cruel and suffocating. Her father had been a military officer in the court of the last Korean emperor and continued to resist the Japanese occupation. As a result, when Sunim was six years old the Japanese military government seized her family's house, all of their belongings, and their remaining lands. They fled just minutes ahead of the Japanese secret police, with only the clothes they were wearing. The family crossed the Han River and built a dugout hut in the mountains south of Seoul. For a long time, their only food was what they could beg or what had been left behind in the fields after the harvest.

The relentless tightening of the Japanese stranglehold on Korea, the collapse of the Korean court, and the pitiful situation of his family filled Sunim's father with despair and frustration. Although her father was always kind and helpful to other people, for some reason he poured out all of his anger and frustration onto Sunim, his eldest daughter. Confused and unable to understand what was happening, Sunim stayed away from the hut as much as possible. Although the darkness and the strange sounds of the night filled her with fear, Sunim began sleeping in the forest, covering herself with leaves to stay warm.

By the time Sunim was eight years old, these days of hunger and cold had lasted for about two years. Although her life had been quite hard, inside Sunim had begun to feel very different. The fear she had felt from being out in the mountains at night had faded, and the dark night had gradually become comfortable, warm, and beautiful. Inside the forest there was no difference between rich and poor, superior and inferior; within the forest, all lives supported each other and lived together harmoniously. In comparison, the world outside seemed to be filled with inequality and suffering.

Everywhere she looked, it seemed as if people were just born to suffer. They spent their days cut off from each other, in the pursuit of things that ultimately seemed so trivial, as if they were just passing the time until they became sick and died. Was this all there was to life? What was the point of such an existence? Intuitively, she sensed that there was something more, something fundamental that her eyes weren't showing her. But what was it? For entire days she would lean against rocks or trees, thinking about these questions, desperately wanting to know and see that which had made her. As she grew older, this desire became so strong that sometimes she felt that it would be better to just die than go on without knowing the answers to these questions. In the midst of this questioning, the forest was a source of peace and comfort that sustained her.

One day she suddenly found what she had been searching for: it was already within her, and had always been within her. It was so warm and wonderful that she called it *appa*, which means "Daddy." This wasn't the father whom she didn't dare let see her, the father who seemed to have no love at all for her; it was the inherent nature that made her, her true nature, the true doer. She cried and cried, calling out "Daddy! Daddy!" filled with joy at knowing that her true parent, her inherent nature, had always been with her.

Years later Kun Sunim laughed about this, saying, "If I hadn't been so young and uneducated, I might have called it Buddha-nature or true self, but at that time all I knew was that it was completely full of love and warmth, so I just called it 'Daddy.' I took the 'Daddy' that I felt within me as my father." From that time on, even though she didn't exactly understand what it was, Sunim took "Daddy" as her place of comfort and poured all of her love into there. Whenever she silently called "Daddy," she felt as if all the rocks, trees, animals and everything else became close friends, so close that it seemed as if they were all breathing as one.

Somehow Sunim knew that "Daddy" could answer all of her questions, and so she just completely relied upon it. She just did so naturally and never tried to rely upon things outside of her. It seemed so amazing to Sunim, that she who had nothing was given the infinite taste of the Dharma.

Sunim felt that "Daddy," her inherent nature, was more precious than anything else in the entire world, and kept insisting, "I want to see you." In response, the thought arose from deep within her: "Look in a mirror, I am there." No matter how many times or how long she looked in the mirror, the only thing she saw was her own face. Nothing else. She was completely baffled. She had never heard any Dharma talks or studied any sutras, and couldn't understand what she was experiencing. Later Sunim recalled, "Even though I was around eighteen years old at that time, I still didn't understand the true meaning of that."

After Korea was liberated in 1945, Sunim followed her inner voice and headed to the Odae mountains. In those mountains was a great *seon*[2] master she had met, called Hanam Sunim.

She had met Hanam Sunim many years before, as a small girl. She had been staying with her uncle who lived in the area, and would often go Hanam Sunim's temple to visit him. Daehaeng Sunim recalled, "I had no idea of the titles he was known by, such as 'Great Sunim,' 'Great Seon Master,' and 'Supreme Wisdom.' He was the head of the entire Jogye Order, but he would play games with me and sneak me toasted rice snacks when nobody was looking. He gave love and compassion to those who were poor and suffering because they were poor and suffered. To those whose eyes shone with their desire to find the truth, he gave wisdom and encouragement. Whoever you were, you could meet him. His words sounded very ordinary, but they always contained a very deep taste. In his deep enlightenment, he was warm and peaceful, like 'Daddy'."

After arriving at the Odae mountains, Sunim became a *haengja*[3] and entered a nearby meditation hall for *Bhikshuni*[4] sunims. After spending several days sitting in meditation, she felt like her knees were being torn apart. Suddenly, a thought arose, "Why am I destroying the cart like this? Instead, why not pull the cow?" As Sunim later explained, "Think of a cart and the cow that pulls it. If you want to go forward, should you hit the cart? No, just take the cow by its nose ring and gently lead it forward."

So she left the meditation hall and returned to the forest. She was so intense in her practice that to her there were no such things as keeping precepts or not keeping precepts, shaving off her hair or having long hair—there was only going inward.

In the spring of 1950, Sunim was ordained as a *Samini*.[5] Hanam Sunim, who was again cutting Sunim's hair, asked, "Right now, who is being ordained?"

Sunim answered, "There is no moment of you giving ordination, and there is no moment of me being ordained. A crane just flies over a blue mountain."

Hanam Sunim said, "You should die, then you will see your-self."

Sunim answered, "Where is the self who should die, and where is the self who should kill?"

He asked further, "Where is your mind?"

Sunim answered, "You must be thirsty. Please have some water."

Finally Hanam Sunim asked, "If I were a magnet, and you were a nail, what would happen?"

Sunim answered, "The nail will also become a magnet."

Hanam Sunim was very pleased, "Outstanding! Now go your own way."

Shortly after this, the Korean War broke out and the country plunged into chaos. Within a few months Hanam Sunim peacefully left his body. He was 75 years old, and had been a disciple of the Buddha for over 50 years.

After leaving Hanam Sunim, Daehaeng Sunim made her way to Busan, where she spent the next year or so. She started a small restaurant for dockworkers and poor people, and also worked as a seamstress, using the fabric from army clothes to make civilian clothes. Previously when Sunim experienced hardships, she had been the only one who suffered, so it hadn't really bothered her. But now it was almost unendurable, seeing the terrible suffering of everyone around her. Although she was able to feed and clothe many people, the feeling began to grow within her that there was a limit to how much she could help people through material means.

Sunim realized that she had to go deeper into her practice, so she left Busan and the life she had created for herself there. Not content with what she had already understood, she kept asking herself, "What's the purpose of life? Why do people have to suffer like this? Why am I here?" She would continuously practice for days and nights without eating or drinking, but the only answer was "You should die, then you will see yourself." She had already solved this question at many deep levels, but she knew she had to go deeper still.

All of Sunim's energy was focused solely on this question as her feet took her around the country. She wanted to know the answer to this question intensely, but still nothing came from inside. Her desire to know the ultimate answer to "You should die and then you will see yourself" was so great that she could feel no value in a life devoid of this answer. As a result, she tried to kill herself several times, but failed each time. Sunim walked without any destination. Her only thought was that she should die someplace where nobody would have to bother with her body. Her feet stopped at the edge of a cliff that overlooked the Han River. But the moment she looked down at the water, she forgot all about dying. She may have spent half a day standing there, looking at the water. Suddenly awakening from this samadhi, her tears flowed uncontrollably. She had realized that "My tears have to be the tears that can become an ocean, an ocean that I will completely drink up."

She was crying tears of joy, for now she had clearly understood how she had to go forward. Her tears were not just tears of simple empathy, rather, they were the tears that arose from truly becoming one with people's suffering and hardships. Furthermore, Sunim now knew that after becoming one with them she had to be able to manifest nondually from the state where she, the foundation, and the one who was suffering were all one. In this way she would be able to truly help both individuals and even the planet.

Sunim spent ten more years in the mountains. She never compared herself to anyone else, and was never content to settle for what she had realized. Instead, she just kept going forward while trying to sincerely apply and experiment with what she had realized, without clinging to any experience or understanding.

Always practicing through mind and testing her understanding and experiences, she was completely unconcerned about her body. When she felt that she should eat something, she just ate whatever plants and grasses were nearby. Sometimes she found wild fruit or mushrooms, and once a farmer gave her some dried beans. She spent several winters under pine trees or in a hole dug in the sand near a river, and during some of those winters the only clothes she had to wear were a light set of summer clothes. Her skin was badly cracked and bleeding, her bones could be clearly seen under her skin, and her hair was tied up in a ball using an arrowroot vine. But people who met her were struck by how bright her eyes were.

Throughout the years of Sunim's practice, it seemed to others that she experienced much suffering, but she never thought of her practice as such. She wasn't intentionally trying to engage in some sort of physical hardship, it was just that all of her attention was directed only toward her true nature.

For Sunim, there was no such thing as letting go or not letting go. She simply put all of her awareness on the foundation that made her. She did not pay any attention to outside things: she just kept watching only what touched her mind inside. It was like sitting quietly in a grassy field and just watching with a peaceful mind. For about a year even the effort of thinking bothered her, so even if questions arose, she did not struggle with them. While practicing like this, sometimes the solution would suddenly arise and sometimes it would come much later.

As Sunim practiced, questions would arise from inside, such as "Why is one of your feet bigger than the other?" But when she looked down at her feet, they were both the same size! When such questions arose, she thought about them very deeply, without noticing whether it was getting dark or not, or how cold it was. She wasn't intentionally practicing that way, it just happened naturally; Sunim wasn't even aware of her body. Although her eyes were closed, inside her mind was clear and bright. One time she spent several days without moving, and afterward her whole body was so stiff that she couldn't even move her hands or feet.

Sunim recalled, "Although I collapsed near death dozens of times, I did not die. I did not starve to death, and did not freeze to death, and I was not hurt by animals. When I was near death, a thought would arise about where I should go to find what I needed. Once, when I was walking at night, suddenly I couldn't move my legs; it was as if they were frozen. When I looked around, I realized that I was just one step away from the edge of a cliff. Do you know what caused my legs to freeze up like that? Things like this happened so many times. I knew that this wasn't a coincidence."

Sunim spoke about these experiences during a Dharma talk: "It was my true self who did all of these things. It was my true self who herded me toward dangerous situations, and it was also my true self who kept me from dying. I was never injured or harmed while living in the mountains and forests even though I was a small and weak woman. I survived like this for more than ten years, even though I never took food with me or prepared clothes for winter. It was all due to the power of *Juingong*."[6]

Sunim once said, "What I experienced toward the end of those ten years cannot be described. Even if I talk about it, no one will believe me. One time a huge dragon transformed into a thousand different shapes; it was so spectacular. Many *mani-jewels*[7] came out from the dragon's mouth, and all of them were connected by a string. I suddenly felt that the dragon was not a dragon. Instead, it was the manifestation of a single thought from the foundation. After this, the dragon soared into the sky, and made a huge column of fire. The character 卍 [8] could be seen lying flat on top of the column of fire. The whole column started to rotate slowly, and it felt as if everything around me were connected to and rotating with this column."

By testing what she had experienced so far, Sunim confirmed the invisible energy of the universe and refined her ability to use it. She felt like she could hold the birth and life of the entire universe in one hand. She began to explore the planets, the solar system, the galaxy, and beyond our galaxy. Sunim also paid special attention to diseases, having seen so much suffering caused by them. She would experiment with using the ability of mind to cure the diseases of villagers who lived in the area, and later would check to see how the disease had been affected. She experimented like this with not only diseases, but also with the family and social problems she observed.

Later while Sunim was still in the mountains, she experienced a huge light. She had been sitting in meditation and was suddenly surrounded by an incredible brightness. The light extended for kilometers in all directions and she felt an indescribable sense of peace and fulfillment. Every direction was filled with light, and it seemed like the light filled even the tiniest of spaces. After this experience, the light always surrounded her and she felt like all things and lives were helping her.

Sunim said, "I never practiced with the intention to become a Buddha or to achieve enlightenment. I just wanted to know who I am, what I am, and why I was born. After realizing that my physical body is not me, my consciousness is not me, and my will is not me, I just wanted to know who I truly was after all of those other things were gone."

Someone once asked Daehaeng Sunim what she obtained while practicing in the mountains. Sunim answered, "Most people think there is some concrete stage that is reached when mind is brightened. However, in fact, 'Nothing to obtain' is the principle that is truly obtained. If you say that you have obtained, have reached, have awakened to something, then already you have not obtained, not reached, and not awakened. Nothing to obtain, nothing to reach, and nothing to awaken to is the way to obtain, to reach, and to awaken."

Another person asked Sunim whether, in order to awaken, they also needed to practice in the mountains as she did. Sunim answered, "Of course not. The most important thing is to practice through mind, not through the body. I just practiced with whatever confronted me, and those happened to be my circumstances. I was poor and didn't have any place to go, so I just practiced like that. Regardless of your circumstances, you have to practice through mind."

Around the end of the 1950s, Daehaeng Sunim stayed in a small hut that was a few hundred meters below Sangwon Temple in the Chiak Mountains. Sunim spent the next ten years there and in the area around the city of Wonju helping whomever she met and gaining many different kinds of experiences. As word spread that she was staying there, many people came to see her, asking for help with their problems. When they spoke of their suffering, she took it on as her own. She listened and only said, "I understand. It will be all right." The people left knowing that their problems would soon be resolved.

They came to see Daehaeng Sunim seeking help with the problems they faced, but sooner or later another problem would always arise. Although she took care of each particular problem, she could see that this didn't fundamentally help them. So, she began to explore ways of teaching people to rely upon their own Buddha-nature, their inherent nature, and to show them that their Buddha-nature was the one that could lead them and take care of all their problems. In this way they could leave the bonds of samsara and karma behind and live freely.

So, in 1972 Daehaeng Sunim moved to Anyang City, just south of Seoul, and established the first *Hanmaum*[9] Seon Center.

There she began to teach people about their own true nature and how to rely on that nature. Many people felt attracted to Daehaeng Sunim's teachings because she showed them how they could practice in everyday life, regardless of how busy they were, what kind of job they had, or what their family situation was like. As time went by, people from more distant areas began asking Daehaeng Sunim to start a Hanmaum Seon Center in their area. In this way, as of 2007, fifteen branches have been established within Korea, and ten Hanmaum Seon Centers have been established overseas. Daehaeng Sunim is also the teacher of more than 180 sunims, many of whom help maintain the centers and assist people who come to the centers.

PART ONE: PRINCIPLES

CHAPTER 1: FUNDAMENTAL QUESTIONS

WHO AM I?

Above all else, you have to truly know yourself. "Who am I?" and "What am I?" are the most important questions there are. You may think, "I'm me. What else would I be?" But it is not that simple. How did you come into existence? If you say that your parents gave birth to you, this implies that you are merely the biological combination of your parents' sperm and ovum. Is this all you are? No, there is that which is your foundation and your root, your true nature. Would you reject your root just because you can't see it? Experiencing your root for yourself is the work you have to do as a human being.

Everything in your life happened after you were born. The world came into being, your family came into being, and every single thing you encounter also came into existence. The entire universe came into existence after you were born. If you didn't exist, what meaning would truth and this world have for you? What is it that hears, sees, sits, stands, speaks, and responds to any situation at any time and place? You must clearly know your true nature, your true root and seed.

The physical body is a kind of shell, but there is something else that moves it. Nevertheless, many people feel that the physical body is truly "me." However, this self is, in fact, like a burlap sack. When the body becomes worn out and is ready to

be thrown away, what use are the things that you have col-
lected as "Mine" during your lifetime?

Notice that your flesh is not eternal, but fleeting, like the
clothes you change. Observe that your thoughts are also like
this. While observing, you must clearly know that what's called
"I" is an insubstantial, temporary existence. Know that this "I"
cannot be free from suffering, and will be destroyed while suffering—but is this everything? No. There is true self, the one
in charge that takes off old clothes and puts on new clothes.

WHAT IS BUDDHA?

The word "Buddha" is often designated as an enlightened person, but Buddha does not depend upon the existence of
enlightened people. Truth does not depend upon the existence
of the teachings of an enlightened person. Although those
teachings are the best way to find true mind, truth is truth no
matter whether there is an enlightened person or not. Even
the word "Buddha" is just a word; you have to find out for yourself what it truly means. This is why Shakyamuni Buddha said,
"Light the Dharma lamp by lighting your inherent lamp."

Buddha embraces every single thing without any trace of "I"
or "I did…". If Buddha, Bodhisattvas, and enlightened beings
occupied a high position, they would never be able to take care
of all aspects of the Dharma realm. The true Buddha can never
be perceived by unenlightened beings' intellect or physical
eyes. It does not have any shape or form, so it cannot be compared to anything else. No seon masters, patriarchs, great
sunims, enlightened people, Bodhisattvas, or Buddhas can be
completely relied upon, because there is no Buddha inside the
word "Buddha." But anyone who awakens to the truth can see
Buddha everywhere.

Buddha is within your *mind*.[10] All beings, patriarchs, enlightened people, and the Buddha who embraces the universe and

encompasses the past, present, and future—all of these are within your mind. Even all of your ancestors are within your mind. What is outside of yourself that you are trying so hard to find?

Because you exist, Buddha exists. Buddha's shape is your shape, and Buddha's mind is your mind.

WHAT IS BUDDHA-NATURE?

Buddha-nature is your fundamental, eternal life, and is the foundation that encompasses the entire universe. However, most people don't realize that this foundation is already within them. If you awaken to the Buddha-nature that is within you, at that instant you become a Buddha.

Buddha-nature existed before heaven and earth were born. It cannot disappear and cannot die, even if the universe collapses and space itself disappears.

Buddha-nature encompasses all visible and invisible phenomena in the universe, and Buddha-nature is within each human being. Thus, within each one of us, there is the inherent ability that is taking care of all things, both seen and unseen.

There is Buddha-nature in every life, and every life is inherently Buddha. Often people think that they can find Buddha-nature at some new and far away place, after crossing distant rivers and mountains, and experiencing all kinds of hardships, but that is not true. The true treasure is within you.

It is possible to become a Buddha even though you do not know anything. Anyone can become a Buddha. If the true treasure were hidden someplace far away and difficult to get to, how could we say that everyone has the same Buddha-nature as the Buddha? The truth that the Buddha taught applies to everyone and everything.

WHAT IS BUDDHA-DHARMA?

The Buddha-Dharma is the truth and principles by which all realms operate. This includes all seen and unseen realms, and all of the beings within them. It is the truth that all Buddhas have awakened to and taught since time immemorial.

The Buddha-Dharma shows us the purpose of life and teaches us the path. If we don't know who we are, then we don't know what to rely upon, or even why to live. The Buddha-Dharma shows us who we are and what life is.

The Buddha-Dharma will never decline as long as human beings exist, because it functions throughout every single part of our daily life. The Buddha-Dharma will never decline as long as life exists, because it functions throughout the daily life of every creature. The Buddha-Dharma will never decline as long as *the three realms*[11] exist, because the functioning of the three realms is itself the Buddha-Dharma. To look at this another way, "Buddha" is the eternal life that every form of existence has, and "Dharma" is the thoughts and actions of those lives.

It is said that it is not easy to meet the essence of the Buddha-Dharma, even over millions of kalpas, not because the Buddha-Dharma is difficult to understand, but because people's minds make it difficult. Although there are many highly regarded and difficult teachings in the world, the Buddha-Dharma is great not because it is highly regarded or difficult, but because it is simple and it easily shows the truth to everyone.

WHAT IS BUDDHISM?

Buddhism functions everywhere and encompasses everything without any limitation. Let's examine the Korean word for Buddhism, *Bulgyo*. The first syllable, *Bul*, refers to the fundamental source of every single life, including even a blade of grass, and the second syllable, *gyo*, refers to learning from each other; we communicate with each other through speech, mind, and actions. So the word "Buddhism" means communicating with each other through the foundation, the fundamental source of life, and through that, listening to each other and learning from each other. "Buddhism" is a description of how the entire universe functions and is also an explanation of the truth itself. No matter the religion, ultimately, its essential teachings are that the foundation of everything exists inside, not outside.

The purpose of studying Buddhism is to discover who I am. Discovering who I am means returning to my foundation. Practicing Buddhism is believing in my true self, not the "I," the label, that I have mistaken for my essence. When we forget this "I," then our true self, which has always existed, will shine through.

CHAPTER 2: ETERNAL TRUTH

HANMAUM

Han means "one," "infinite," and "combined," and *ma-um* means "mind." So *Hanmaum* means "the fundamental mind that is intangible, invisible, beyond time and space, and has no beginning or end." It means that all minds, and all beings, the world, and the universe are all interconnected and are working together as one. In other words, Hanmaum embraces the whole universe and all the lives within it.

Every single life and thing in the universe has Buddha-nature, which has existed without beginning, exists now, and will exist forever. Buddha-nature is only one, so it is Hanmaum; it is inconceivably large, so it is Hanmaum; it is not an individual thing, but the interconnected whole, in which all things are working together, so it is Hanmaum. All things come from it, so it is Hanmaum.

The minds of all lives in the world are one. Fundamentally, there is no "you" or "I" separating them. Inherently, life is one. Inherently, life is Buddha. The minds of all lives are working together as one, so this is called "one mind," Hanmaum. Although each life has its own separate physical body, inherently, they are not two.

The entire universe is directly connected to the fundamental mind of humans and all life. Everything that functions and moves in the world is already directly connected to our foundation. Everything in the whole universe, including both the visible and invisible realms, is connected and communicates as one. Nothing exists apart from anything else: the mind of all Buddhas is your inherent mind, and the Dharma of all Buddhas is the Dharma of your inherent mind and your daily life. Hanmaum connects all things as one, just as the same electricity brightens this light bulb and that one.

JUINGONG

Juingong is the fundamental mind with which each one of us is inherently endowed, and the mind that is directly connected to every single thing. Through this connection, Juingong functions together with everything as one.

Juingong is my true foundation. My body and my thoughts are like branches and leaves that arise and disappear. Juingong is the root that makes new branches and leaves when the old ones break and fall. If I am the fruit, Juingong is the stem that sustains the fruit. If I am a stem, Juingong is the branch from which the stem hangs. If I am a branch, Juingong is the trunk that the branch comes from. If I am the trunk, Juingong is the root; the root is the basis of the tree—the trunk, branches, leaves, and fruit all come from it. Like this, all of my thoughts, all of my activities and all of my *virtue and merit*[12] arise from Juingong.

Why is it called Juingong? It is the doer, so it is called "Ju-in (主)," and it is completely empty, that is, it is always changing, without any fixed shape, so it is called "Gong (空)." Thus Juingong means your fundamental, underlying essence, which is always changing and manifesting. Your existence is based upon Juingong. What were you before you were born from your parents? A human being is not just the combination of a sperm and ovum; Juingong also has to combine together with these. Your life and Juingong are like a tree that is able to live because of its root. However, don't think of Juingong as something fixed and stationary, like a tree root. Juingong is your foundation and the doer of everything, so it can also be called "Buddha." Thus if you awaken to Juingong, you will also know what Buddha truly is.

You can call Juingong "Dad" or "Mom." Also, you can call it "the owner of mind," "ordinary mind," "pure water," "life-giving water," or "the pillar of mind." You can call Juingong "one thing" or "inherent nature." You can call Juingong "the thing that does not have anything," or you can call it "Amida Buddha," or "the main Buddha."[13] You can call it "God" or "my love" because it is the fundamental place. Juingong can never be fixed because it can become anything. Juingong is the parent as well as the child, the highest person as well as the lowest. Juingong is the true self that leads you, no matter what name is used. Juingong is "the true essence of me" and "the mind of my mind."

Juingong was never born and will never die. Juingong is the eternal and vast true self, which cannot be seen with physical eyes and cannot be caught by thought. It will never weaken or disappear because it is absolutely pure and because it has the great power of bright wisdom. It is the true self that has infinite ability. Unenlightened beings exist in different forms, with different names, at different levels, and they are born and die. However, Juingong is also called "Buddha" or "inherent Buddha" because it is just as it is, even as one becomes ten thousand and ten thousand become one. Through Juingong, unenlightened beings and Buddha meet, and they are not two.

Juingong doesn't exist someplace else. It is found in the person who is willing to look for it. When we cook, we prepare the ingredients, combine them, and make a delicious meal. Like this, while living as you want and need to, the true nature of Juingong is revealed in your daily life.

Juingong is a giant furnace. It is the furnace that always works together with all Buddhas' deep and sincere spiritual power, which encompasses all visible and invisible realms. This furnace is inside you. Like iron melting in a furnace, this furnace changes all tears to compassion, and all pain is reborn as feelings of gratitude. Any kind of disaster or painful karma is just a snowflake in front of it. Juingong is the mysterious and profound secret of mind, which everyone is endowed with, and it is the incredible power of Buddha-nature, which every life has. This is the majestic virtue of Juingong.

You should not think of Juingong as some kind of separate, individual self that belongs to you alone. Juingong means the whole. Juingong embraces and sustains everything in the universe, and takes care of everything in all of the visible and invisible realms. This is Juingong. How could it be divided into my Juingong and your Juingong?

MY TRUE REALITY

Flesh, Consciousness, and the Foundation

A human being is the result of three things: the eternal foundation combined together with the flesh, and consciousness. These three work together harmoniously.

The state before thoughts arise, the act of giving rise to thoughts, and the body are all working together as one. This is called "functioning as one mind."

The essence of Juingong is in the working together of our eternal foundation, consciousness, and the flesh. These three share all things together, help each other, and live as one. This Juingong is endowed with the ability to send out and bring in everything. The visible self is a physiological tool of the invisible self. Juingong is formless and intangible, but it is the essence that moves us.

At the point where our eternal foundation, the perceptions

that give rise to thought, and the body all intersect, these three
function together and manifest into the world. As these three
function together harmoniously, they manifest as a wise guide,
as my teacher.

The Physical Body and the Four Elements

Our body is only a temporary combination. Earth, water, fire,
and air gather together and form our body. They gather according to *karmic affinity*,[14] and later they scatter according to karmic
affinity. Thus, time after time, you've experienced birth and
death. Anything subject to birth and death cannot be called
true reality. If it is not true reality, the changeless essence, which
is never born, and never disappears, then it is merely an illusion.
The physical body has often been called an illusion because it,
too, is a temporary combination.

As clouds gather together, dissolve, and gather again to form
different clouds, a human body will one day disappear and
return to its elements. Then, according to the circumstances,
the four elements will gather again and take another form.
However, do not let the idea that your body will scatter into
the four elements make you feel that everything is pointless.
Instead, you should understand the principle that everything
scatters and then gathers together again. Practitioners of the
Buddha-Dharma don't see our existence as futile, because they
realize that the very impermanence of the world enables them
to awaken to the truth.

If living beings are only a temporary combination, then
where is true self, Juingong? Does it exist apart from this temporary combination? No, it does not. Juingong does not exist
separately from what is called the false self. Then where is your
true self? In the arms? In the legs? In the heart? In the brain? It
does not exist in any of those places. You cannot find anything
that you could call true self by observing the body, but

nonetheless, it exists within you. Juingong, your true self, is the basis of the false self. Your true self forms your physical body and interacts with the Buddha realm. In all of this, the workings of your inherent nature, Juingong, are the manifestation of truth itself. It is so mysterious and profound!

There has to be a physical body in order to know the Buddha-Dharma. You need to know that throwing away your body is not the way to know the Buddha-Dharma. To think that the flesh is worthless and must be thrown away because it is only a temporary combination is an extremely misguided idea. Without the body, you cannot develop, cannot broaden your wisdom, and cannot become a Buddha. Because the son exists, you can know that the father also exists; because the servant exists, you realize that the master must also exist. By understanding visible phenomena, you can come to understand the invisible essence, the non-material foundation that gives rise to and animates all visible phenomena, and which always works together as one with all things.

Because the tree exists, you can know the root; because the fruit exists, you can know the seed. Likewise, even though the body is only a temporary, karmic combination of the four elements, through it you can know the fundamental place, Hanmaum Juingong, which is the source of all life and all phenomena.

My True Nature

Where did we come from? We came from Juingong, our true self, so we have to find our true self. As we have evolved through life after life, true self has always been with us. However, we won't know this unless we try to find it. Realize that everything comes from true self. The physical body is like the leaves or the branches that come from the root, the true self. How could you forget about the root, and call the branches and leaves "me"? Know the root!

It is said that being born is the combination of your father's bones and your mother's flesh, together with your life and mind, which have passed through millions of kalpas. When "I," the unenlightened illusion of self, is completely forgotten, there is something eternal. It is Juingong, the eternal self that was never born and will never die. It is the self that is never stained, and which transcends all suffering. It is the self that is precious and blissful beyond comparison, that is never born or disappears, that never increases or decreases, and is never dirty or clean. But ordinary people are not able to meet this eternal self because they can't escape from the prison of their own concepts. The eternal self cannot be described by words, and it cannot be revealed through discussion. Trying to know it conceptually is like trying to know the world while trapped inside of a barrel.

From a very long time ago, people raised upside-down, dream-like thoughts. These became a darkness that obscured Hanmaum, which is inherently bright and clear. It is like the bright sun and clear sky being hidden by clouds. The sun and the sky have been hidden by darkness for so long that people forgot they ever existed. What unenlightened people must do is to return to their true nature, which is inherently Buddha, the sun, and the sky. Even your present thoughts and body are just one spot of gray cloud that has arisen from inherent self. There is no substance to the "I" that people have thought of as themselves. However, it is said that "I" has no substance, not because such reality does not exist, but because what is called "I" always changes from moment to moment.

NON-DUALITY

When waves occur in the sea, many drops of water are created. However, when they sink, they all become the water of the sea itself. In this case, the drops can be compared to living beings, and the sea can be compared to the fundamental place. A small drop of water being created is like a life being born. A small drop sinking is like a life taking off its body and returning to the foundation. Like this, at the fundamental place there is no division of "you" and "I." There is no division between your ancestors and my ancestors. The foundation of life is vast and huge, but it is one. It exists like the calm water of the sea, and according to circumstances, it manifests as large or small. Like drops of water that are created and disappear according to the wind, our bodies arise and disappear.

Because all things are interconnected and functioning as one, the foundation of the universe is the foundation of my mind. Because nothing is separate, we can manifest non-dually, so there is nothing that is not myself.

From the perspective of the phenomenal world, everything exists separately, but from the perspective of the foundation, everything is one. Fundamentally, all things are one, but in appearance they are separate. Thus, it is said that mountains are mountains, and water is water.

Even this body is not "mine." It is a community. Across the Earth, there are many kinds of animals. Likewise, inside my body there are many different kinds of lives. Hence, although it is my body, it is not "mine," it is a community. Unenlightened people usually think that they own their physical body, but even within each of the organs—the heart, liver, stomach, and so on—there are several hundred millions of lives, and they all function together automatically. This body is like a small universe, and like a universe, all of the body's parts function together as one. And in this body are contained all sciences and philosophies.

CAUSE AND EFFECT

The universe and the human world are interconnected and work together as one. In our body, uncountable numbers of cells are connected together like a huge net. In the same way, the Earth and the entire universe are thoroughly and systematically connected, like a well-made net, functioning together as one. Therefore, if I know something, the Dharma realm and Buddha also know it—the entire universe knows it.

Because you know what you did, all of the beings within your body know what you did, so Hanmaum, the universe, and the Dharma realm also know. Because all things and lives are interconnected, nothing you do is secret.

A lie is you deceiving yourself. The one who deceives and the one who is deceived is you. You can never deceive Juingong. Juingong is the sky, the universe, and the Dharma realm—there is nothing that can be hidden from it.

Mind can be compared to a supercomputer. Any thought, once raised, is perfectly recorded. You might believe that a thought is finished because you are no longer aware of it, but that thought did not disappear. Rather, it is perfectly recorded inside of your mind. The thought is stored in the subconscious and causes a similar thought to arise next time. Further, the second thought is stronger than the first thought. For example, if the first thought was bad, then the second thought is often a little worse. In this way, the thought keeps repeating time after time and grows stronger and stronger. Mind is tilted toward the thoughts that arise often. So, if you do not manage your thoughts well, they will grow and eventually become actions.

If mind moves and raises a thought once, that thought is perfectly recorded; the functioning of mind is not limited to just our conscious awareness.

Good karma is also karma. Once something is recorded, that record tends to push people around and control them. Bad karma gives birth to bad results, and good karma gives birth to good results. Karma is what leads beings through the cycle of birth and death, so there is no difference between good karma and bad karma. In one case, a slave suffers because he or she meets a bad master. In another case, a slave lives relatively comfortably because he or she meets a good master. However, both are the same, both are slaves.

If you record over a tape recording, the previous recording is erased and the new material is recorded. So it's better to record good karma rather than bad karma. However, instead of just recording good karma, it's even better to completely erase all of the recordings. The way to do this is by entrusting everything that confronts you, both good and bad, to your fundamental nature. It's like cleaning a mirror. Even though the mirror has been covered by dust for a long time, once you wipe it, it immediately becomes clean.

The law of causality is like a seed that never rots: once planted, it always sprouts. If you plant a good seed, good results will follow. If you plant a bad seed, bad results will occur. Cause and effect are like seeds that always sprout. Further, once planted they will sprout, go to seed, and then sprout again and again.

There are lots of people who live without any concern for others. They're satisfied as long as they are happy and can do or get what they want. But you cannot obtain true peace by making yourself alone comfortable. Temporary enjoyment cannot solve the fundamental problem. You must know that our life does not end with this present life. Furthermore, you must know that everything, even the things that you have done secretly, comes back to you as karma.

Karma is a tangle of uncountable causes and effects. Some people try to use their intellect to unravel their karma, but this is like trying to melt a frozen lake in winter by pouring one bucket of hot water onto the ice. It seems to melt a little, but before long the water you poured freezes, and you have only added more ice. So don't get caught up in worldly things, release them all to your fundamental mind, and let them melt down automatically. When spring comes, the frozen lake will melt naturally and completely. Returning to your fundamental mind is like a warm spring coming after a cold winter.

There is no such thing as fate or destiny. Everything depends upon your mind. Because you are not free from attachments, those attachments become karma and even affect your genes. Because everything is done by mind, the key to happiness or unhappiness is how you use your mind.

THE PRINCIPLE OF EVOLUTION

Samsara[15] and Rebirth

Being born and dying is samsara, and growing old is also samsara. The coming and going of the seasons is also samsara. A drop of water circulates and feeds and sustains infinite lives: this is also samsara. The birth and disappearance of the stars is also samsara. All things and all lives are endlessly coming and going like this. They don't just disappear after having lived. If there were no such cycle of samsara, how could anyone ever learn about truth?

In order to be born as a human being, it may have taken a thousand years of accumulated virtue and merit. It's so hard to become a human being. Nevertheless, if you don't let go of the habits you developed prior to becoming a human being, and if you think of only yourself, your suffering will be endless. If you live this way, you may live like this for many, many lives, stuck like a hamster on a wheel, unable to evolve. Or you may devolve and be reborn as an animal. Once you are reborn as an animal, you will suffer a lot, having to eat others or be eaten. There will be very little opportunity to reflect upon your state, and if you develop the habits of an animal, it will be even more difficult to free yourself from that state, even over billions of kalpas, billions of eons.

There are some people who think of the cycle of birth and death as inescapable suffering, but those people who have awakened understand that samsara is just the process of manifestation. For those people who do not know that all things and all lives manifest and work together while always changing and never standing still for even a second, it will be rebirth and suffering. However, when they awaken, it is only manifestation.

Without samsara, there would be no evolution. Samsara is the power with which you can become Buddha. Thus, samsara is not suffering caused by karma: samsara is the process of evolution and makes spiritual practice possible. Even at this very moment, we are endlessly dying and being born. Because you died in the past, you can live today. Living and dying always accompany each other like this and happen together. Therefore, inside of death, life already exists, and inside of life, death already exists. Samsara, this continuous and endless changing of all things, is the power that shapes and polishes you and makes you a Buddha. It would not be possible to become a Buddha without samsara.

Death is when the unchangeable foundation of mind, Juingong, changes clothes. When our clothes are worn out, we replace them with new clothes. Like this, Juingong replaces a worn-out body with a fresh one. Thus, death is just getting ready to put on a set of new clothes.

Even after your body falls away, your consciousness remains. It often happens that people do not understand that their body does not exist anymore, and they do not realize that living people cannot see or hear them. So, sometimes, in their confusion and desire, they cause other people to suffer. If you sincerely cultivate mind while you have a body, then you can leave without having any attachments. However, if you don't practice, then even though you're dead, you'll be caught up in all of your old relationships, and won't be able to freely leave. Instead, you may just wander around as a ghost, stuck in that state for a very long time. When people die, if they have never practiced spiritual cultivation, their consciousness cannot see and cannot hear. In the middle of the darkness, their consciousness cannot correctly perceive things, so those people often enter the womb of a pig or a magpie. However, people who have cultivated mind give off a great light and thoroughly illuminate their surroundings. Even their families tend to live brightly, although individually they may know nothing anything about spiritual practice.

Evolution and Creation

From the perspective of a human being, we may think of some lives as tiny and seemingly worthless. But all existence is in the process of evolution. Thus, they are our past shapes, our old friends, and show us where we have evolved from. When we look at the four types of lives,[16] we see that they have all evolved from microbes, and that they form a progression from the lowest to the highest. However, these four types of lives exist within the body of every single life, and are also evolving within each body. So, how can we say which lives are the most important or which should be the standard for comparison. Look at the world, there is no starting or ending point—there is just the middle path.

From the perspective of the process of evolution, lives are affected by circumstances and the environment, and they can adapt themselves to a certain degree. However, the more fundamental things depend upon consciousness. There are so many truly mysterious things. If we should become dissatisfied with our present shape, and the desire to change becomes strong, then the shape of human beings will begin to change. The shapes of all of existence were formed by mind. What is the power that can do this? It is the true mind, Juingong.

Although lives exist at many different levels, they all have mind. Mind is the owner of the body, like the driver of a car. The body just follows what the mind tells it to do. And that mind hopes to have a better today than yesterday, a better tomorrow than today, and works to accomplish this. Lives are continuously evolving through the virtue arising from that effort.

The completion of evolution is obtaining great freedom and becoming a Buddha of infinite virtue and merit. All lives are in the process of accomplishing this; they are all our brothers and sisters, walking toward the same destination. Thus, all realms are a great school, full of beings who are practicing the way.

Evolution and creation are all manifestations of Hanmaum. Evolution means raising the level of mind. Once the level of mind changes, the body also changes accordingly. Evolution is the process of the mind becoming brighter, while creation is the outward manifestation of the mind's design. Thus, while this process is evolution, it is also creation, and while it is creation, it is also evolution.

Creation is the outward manifestation of the mind's design. However, even when something is created, it's always changing. It doesn't remain the same, with fixed ideas and unchanging behaviors. Thus, creation is manifestation. Mind is the basis of both evolution and creation; they are not two. Devolution is also done by mind. All of these are manifestations of mind.

THE ESSENCE OF TRUTH: MANIFESTATION OF EMPTINESS

Truth is the flowing that never stops for even a moment. It flows, infusing everything, and is alive. There is nothing in the world that is unmoving; there is only flowing. Without beginning or end, without birth or death, there is only flowing, just as it is. This flowing is always fresh and alive. To stop something from flowing is to kill it.

We live inside of truth. As fish live in water, truth permeates our daily life. Trying to find truth far away is like a fish trying to find something outside of water. Truth transcends time and space, and never stands still for even a second. It functions endlessly, like a person continuously breathing in and out. It can be called "endlessly circling a pagoda."[17]

True reality is not inherently hidden; it only appears that way to unenlightened eyes. True reality is inherently crystal clear, like something in bright sunlight, but unenlightened beings do not see it. In fact, you could even say that the essence of the Buddha-Dharma is correctly seeing the true reality of all things. When the Buddha taught the Eightfold Noble Path, he first said, "See correctly." If you see correctly, then you will obtain wisdom. If you have wisdom, then you will attain emancipation. Thus, if unenlightened beings can see correctly, all of the suffering and anguish, irrationality, and conflicts that they face will disappear. This is because they realize that those things are inherently empty, without any roots, while their fundamental nature is eternally bright and profound.

To change every moment means to die every moment. On the other hand, it also means to be reborn every moment. Foolish people cling to moments that have already passed by, and in so doing lead futile lives, whereas wise people, understanding that everything changes each instant, apply this principle to their daily lives, and live freely.

Nothing in the universe remains the same, not even for an instant. There is only change and manifestation, so there is nothing you can carry with you. Thus, when there are no fixed thoughts of "I," even suffering does not exist. Although there is nothing you can carry with you, you think that you carry some burden, and so you bind yourself up with this fixed idea. If you know that everything changes each instant, that everything is empty, then there is nothing for you to cling to. Form is empty, thoughts are empty, words are empty, names and titles are empty—everything is empty.

Which "I" are you? When you are standing, sitting, moving, or staying still, which of these "I"s is really you? The "me" that meets my friends and the "me" that meets my brother are both different. So which one is really me? Is the young "me" myself? Or is the elderly "me" who I truly am? In the same way, there is no stationary "I"; it's impossible to stick a label on anything else in the universe and say "this is...". Thus it has been said that everything is empty, not because there is nothing, but because there is such continuous change and transformation.

Emptiness (空) doesn't mean that there is nothing. Emptiness gives rise to matter, and is not different from matter. Emptiness continuously manifests as matter. While living, it dies; while dead, it lives—it flows and changes without being stationary for even a moment. Emptiness is not dead—it is alive. To be empty means to be full. Because the manifestations and workings of emptiness are so infinite, seon masters often just said "Nothing (無)!" Sometimes even this wasn't enough, so again they said "Nothing!"

Modern science has advanced greatly, but it has now begun to reach limitations that science itself can't overcome. Unless we develop our spiritual level, it will be impossible to overcome these limitations. Without spiritual development, it will gradually become more and more difficult for human beings to survive. This is because material development and spiritual development must occur together at the same time. Emphasis solely on material development is leading human society down a dead end road.

Do matter and material things lead humans? No, all matter and energy are controlled and directed by our fundamental mind. If people don't know this foundation, there is a limit to what science can do. Thus we must take a new approach to science by returning to our fundamental mind and learning to start from there. Our inherent mind is the basis of every field of science. So, although scientists work on all kinds of research, it is only by knowing our fundamental mind that we can continue to develop.

The speed of light is considered to be the fastest thing in the universe, but it is not faster than mind. The ability of mind is such that if you awaken there is nothing you cannot know, and there is no place you cannot reach. Even the wonderful inventions produced by modern science cannot come close to the great power and ability of a Buddha, an awakened one. The limitations facing modern science can be easily overcome if you're able to use the mysterious power of mind. Not only can those who have awakened freely go to realms that exist in higher dimensions, but they can also transcend all dimensions—including space and time.

The Buddha knew that displaying this ability tends to just confuse people, without really helping them, so he was careful about doing such things. If you sincerely believe in the power of mind and awaken, then, while continuing to practice, you will be able to clearly see all of the things that are invisible to ordinary people. The ability of our fundamental mind is the most profound and mysterious thing in the entire universe.

Even though medicine has advanced so much, in reality it isn't able to solve much more than thirty percent of the problems people face. Why is this? Modern science deals with only the phenomenal half of existence, so even at its best it cannot possibly solve more than fifty percent of the problems confronting it. In order for science to understand the whole, it has to be able to understand the unseen half of existence. The only way to do this is through understanding our fundamental mind, and putting that understanding into practice. It will be impossible to perform complete research unless one's latent consciousness and present consciousness combine together and function as one through the fundamental mind.

Not only the Buddha, but also *Dangun*[18] and all other awakened beings have taught humanity the spiritual path by which they can transcend the limitations of material development. As life and death exist at the crossroads of inhaling and exhaling, our current material culture has now advanced to the point where we must change direction and travel the path of the spiritual.

Some scientists are trying to communicate with extraterrestrials by sending signals into space. But the attempt to communicate with extraterrestrials through radio waves shows that these scientists do not know about the foundation. In order to communicate with beings like that, we have to take the material realm, the fifty percent we already know, and step into the spiritual realm, the unseen realm. The path is blocked if you ignore your foundation; through mind you have to activate the wireless telephone that is within you, then the path will be open and you can communicate. If you can break through in this way, there is nothing anywhere that you cannot see, hear, or understand. Furthermore, nothing will be able to block or hinder you. You will become aware of the existence of a completely different style of living. This is what is called the all-reaching hands and feet of Buddha.

From the basic elements, every kind of life arose. Every life has the inherent ability to change, and they have done so, manifesting with every kind of shape over eons and eons. Even though some are born as animals, they don't remain that way forever, and even though some are born as humans, that isn't their permanent shape. All of this is driven by mind.

If a toy top becomes unbalanced, it begins to wobble and can't rotate stably. Likewise, even our galaxy could not maintain a stable orbit if it weren't for the support of something called *mujeonja*. This mujeonja is the bridge that makes it possible to go back and forth between the phenomenal realm and the invisible realm. Further, it is mujeonja that allows the orderly functioning of the principles and laws that govern the phenomenal world.

People say that there is no life on Mars, but how can you say that there's no life there just because you cannot see it? Mars is so crowded with lives. In this middle realm—the Earth—seen and unseen lives are sifted and sorted, and then raised to upper realms or sent down to lower realms. Likewise, every other planet also has its own unique assignment. If you learn to return to and rely upon your fundamental mind, it's like having an owner who looks after the house, so that your spirit can never be stolen, and your ability can never be taken.

The worms crawling in the ground think that the dirt is very wide, but they do not realize how big the sky is. Likewise, human beings create and cling to Earth-type habits because Earth-type life is all they can imagine. They do not know how to see the Earth from the perspective of the universe. Make mind the center of your spiritual practice and learn to step outside of your fixed ideas.

The universe is full of unseen lives. Not only the Earth, but other planets are also crowded with them. In the body, blood circulates through arteries and veins, and the internal organs all perform their own functions. Likewise, galaxies and the Earth are also continuously moving and have their own roles to play in the functioning of the universe. All things in the universe are able to function together harmoniously because there is the fundamental, underlying mind that allows them to rely upon and stabilize each other.

PART TWO: CULTIVATING MIND [19]

CHAPTER 4: THE ESSENCE OF MIND

WHAT IS MIND?

Mind is the foundation of the universe, the foundation of the sun, and the foundation through which human beings manage and do all of the things in their daily lives. Mind is the omniscient and omnipotent creator that makes everything and transcends all concepts.

Mind does not have color, shape, location, beginning, or end. Mind cannot be said to be this or that, inside or outside. Mind cannot be divided, cannot be absorbed, and cannot be destroyed. It transcends time, it transcends space, it transcends everything.

There is mind inside of mind, the fundamental mind, which from the very beginning is absolutely clean, can never be stained, and is as it is. On the other hand, there is also the discriminating mind, which causes us to pass through the cycle of life and death. It doesn't know about the existence of the fundamental mind and thinks that ever-changing defilements and delusions are its essence. For the sake of explanation, we can talk about two different types of mind, but in actuality they are not separate.

People's state of consciousness exists at many different levels, according to the thoughts they give rise to, but underlying all of this is the inherent fundamental mind that is never created and which never disappears. You have to find the mind inside of mind.

Mind is always complete as it is, so it shines forth like the sun. Mind is never hindered by anything—it is always just as it is. Inwardly and outwardly its ability is unlimited. There is no one and no thing that can take it away or destroy it. No matter how powerful a spirit, no matter how great a Buddha, neither one can destroy your fundamental mind. Although the sun is very bright and the universe inconceivably vast, they are not greater than the light and ability of your mind.

All realms and all universes are connected together through the same fundamental mind. Thus, everything shares the same body, same life, works together as one, and shares all things together. Mind can freely come and go without any hindrance, even over distances of thousands or millions of miles. Ultimately, everything and everyone in the universe is harmoniously living together, sharing the same root.

The nature of mind is like a clear and unstained mirror. When something is in front of such a mirror, the mirror reflects every single aspect of the image clearly. But if the object disappears, no trace of it remains on the mirror. Likewise, although mind reflects every single thing, no ripples or stains remain. Without understanding this aspect of mind, people paint all kinds of pictures on the mirror, one on top of another, and end up causing themselves hardships. However, if we return to our inherent nature, which is our most true and natural state, then the true reality of everything is automatically revealed.

No matter how dark clouds may be, they cannot stain the sky. Similarly, bad thoughts or intentions cannot stain your fundamental mind. Even if dark clouds are very thick, eventually they will disappear, and the sky will be blue and clear, as it was before. Even if storm clouds pour rain down, the sky is only covered; behind the clouds, it remains clear and bright. In the same way, even though defilements and delusions may seem very thick, true mind remains clear and bright, and is never stained.

Mind has no hindrance. Inherently, every direction is wide open. Nor are there impregnable silver mountains or iron walls that you have to penetrate. But if mind has no inherent hindrances why is it said that there is something you have to overcome? Because through your thoughts you have built up a wall that blocks you.

You must understand the nature of mind: although mind is intangible, it functions equally and thoroughly throughout all material and non-material realms. Once you realize this, you will understand that there never was any hindrance in the first place.

THE PROFOUND ABILITY OF MIND

When mind is deep and sincere, there is no place it does not reach. Mind is the true energy, the energy with which lives evolve and the world develops. However, unless people believe in the energy of mind, they cannot use it and it cannot manifest in their lives. If you would truly experience this energy for yourself, you must start by realizing it's there.

Mind has the power of magnetism, the power of light, the power of electricity, and the power of communication. This infinite ability of mind brings whatever is needed, communicates with everything everywhere, and freely gives and receives. If you completely let go of the thought "I'm doing...," you can freely use the energy of mind thoroughly and clearly, without being intimidated by anything. If you want to use the energy of mind, you just use it; if you don't want to use it, you don't, without clinging to thoughts of using or not using. You must know that the energy of mind comes from your foundation and functions thoroughly throughout the Dharma realm. Believe in your mind and use it freely.

Every single thing, without exception, hears, speaks, and understands through mind. Thus, when you stand before an image of the Buddha and have a sincere and humble mind, if you know that all Buddhas' minds and your mind are not separate, then you will become one with all Buddhas, and all Buddhas will become one with you.

It is mind that causes people to fall into hell or to go directly to heaven. The thoughts you give rise to, even if only once, can cause you to fall into a deep pit, or they can free you from that pit. However, most people live without realizing how important even a single thought can be. The joys of heaven and the sufferings of hell all depend upon a single thought.

Mind is the most important thing. Mind cannot die: even if the body dies, mind cannot escape from what you have done. So, evolving and awakening your mind is the only thing that is important. It's more important than even your life itself. In spite of this, there are many people who seem to be making deliberate efforts to cause their minds to devolve.

There is a great treasure within your mind. This treasure is like a pearl buried in mud, but it is absolutely there. It is as if you have millions of dollars in a bank account—why would you think you are poor? Why do you think that you have nothing? Spiritual practice means having faith that there is a great treasure within your mind, and then finding it. Learning to discover the treasure within you is the most worthwhile thing in the world. If you can put this into practice, you can live freshly, with a mind open like sky, always overflowing with compassion. What could be better than this?

THE THOUGHTS THAT WE GIVE RISE TO

When we raise a thought for someone's well-being, and entrust that to our foundation, that underlying mind never disappears and is never used up. This is different from helping people through material things. This is the unconditional love that Bodhisattvas have for all beings. This mind is the compassion that rises when all beings and myself are one, when the suffering of others is my suffering. This is the power that leads us to the truth.

Raising a thought from the foundation is not the same as generating a thought with your intellect. A thought from the foundation is naturally free of any sense of the notion "I raised a thought." When you are able to raise this kind of thought, you never lose sight of Juingong, your foundation, for even an instant. Moreover, while letting go and returning to your foundation every kind of suffering and hardship you encounter, you are aware that even letting go is being done by Juingong. When you have this kind of very deep faith, that even the things "you" are doing are actually being done by Juingong,[20] then it can be said that your foundation has come out in front. Thus, the thoughts you give rise to while firmly gripping your foundation will be completely free of concepts like "I did...." However, if you try to raise thoughts from your intellect, you will find your progress blocked.

A thought raised from your foundation is like a middleman: it connects your flesh with your inherent nature. In an instant it can reach anywhere in the universe and Dharma realm. In an instant it can reach the future and the past, and even the realms beyond life. It moves faster than light, so distances of "near" and "far" are meaningless.

People are often careless about the thoughts they give rise to, assuming that once they forget about a thought, that thought is finished. This is not true. Once you give rise to a thought, it keeps functioning and eventually its consequences return to you. It's an automatic process.

Entrusting everything to Juingong, that is, letting go and resting, means returning to your true foundation. Because all things, visible and invisible, come from there, if you return to that foundation and raise a thought, then that thought will manifest in the world. A thought at that moment is like pushing a button that starts everything operating automatically. This is because all things begin with thoughts that have arisen from the foundation. When you entrust everything to the foundation, with a single thought you can go a thousand miles.

Raise thoughts from the place that does not stand still. If you raise thoughts from a place that stands still, that is, from your fixed concepts and ideas, then you will be caught by outside things and you will be a slave to the material world. On the other hand, if you think that you have to ignore outside things, then you have already raised thoughts from a place that stands still, and so you will become a slave to the non-material world. If you sincerely believe in your eternal friend, your Buddha-nature, you will know where you have to raise thoughts from.

The moment negative thoughts arise, strike back. At that moment, change that thought into something positive. "Of course this is possible! Juingong is taking care of it." While observing how what you entrusted to your foundation, to Juin-gong, turns out, you will come to understand the ability of mind, and how profound and mysterious it is.

A single misguided thought can cause people to ruin their bodies and destroy their families. Furthermore, it can also ruin communities, nations, the Earth, and even the whole universe. All beings are one body, one family, one community, one universe. The universe, the Earth, Buddha, and all principles and laws that govern this world are contained within our minds. We have to raise thoughts such that all of the lives within our body function together harmoniously as one. Then the unenlightened lives within our bodies become Bodhisattvas, and our bodies become healthy.

Money coming or going, harmony, wisdom, and health can

all turn upon a single thought. With a single thought, poverty can be overcome; with a single thought, disease can be cured; with a single thought, you can embrace and help others. Because mind is infinite, it can embrace the universe and still have room left over. Thus, if you understand the truth of non-duality, you can completely embrace everything. If you raise one thought that is calm, noble, and humble, and do so without any trace of like or dislike, or of "I," then that thought begins to manifest in the world and becomes medicine for all suffering. All energy will follow and work together with this kind of a thought.

Above all else, you have to believe that you have Buddha-nature, the power within yourself that enables you to become a Buddha. Then, like a gardener taking care of a plant, you have to make this Buddha-nature bloom. However, most people have forgotten about this Buddha-nature. Even though flowers bloom and drop according to the season, everyone knows that there is the power inside of plants to bloom again the following year. But people have forgotten that there is also such ability within themselves. If we can realize that we are at the greatest moment of transformation after having gone through innumerable lives, then we will truly know that inside ourselves there is the power to become a Buddha.

If you do not believe in yourself, you cannot receive the key to mind. How can the key to the treasure storehouse be given to you if you do not believe? You already have every kind of treasure there is, so believe in yourself and throw away those thoughts that you are great or that you are no good. True self can do all things—even things that you imagined were impossible. If you have faith that true self can do it, you can survive even on top of a barren rock. If you believe that Juingong does everything and can resolve everything, then your Juingong instantly manifests as *Avalokiteshvara Bodhisattva*[21] and teaches the Dharma, or manifests as the Medicine Bodhisattva and shows the Dharma. Thus there's no need for calling out "Buddha, help me!" or "Avalokiteshvara Bodhisattva, save me!" All Buddhas and Bodhisattvas, all awakened beings, and all the profound ability and power of the universe exist inside of belief.

Unenlightened people do not know what is truly good and what is not good. Therefore, the best thing for people to do is to strongly believe that Juingong is always taking care of everything. However, many people ask, "What happens if I believe and entrust things to Juingong, but then they don't turn out the way I want them to?" This is not belief. Once you truly have faith, entrusting something takes only an instant, and there's nothing left over for you to worry about. Juingong never ignores your faith. Everything is done through sincere belief; belief is the key.

Belief rewards you in proportion to your faith. It gives everything to those people who wholeheartedly believe, and it gives half to those people who halfheartedly believe. This is why complete belief in Juingong is emphasized. Don't be discouraged when hardships confront you. Even if hardships arise from your foundation, as long as you have faith, your foundation can also solve those problems.

When you have unwavering faith that "Juingong can solve it," you begin to find your true self. When you have strong faith like this, you will be free from fear and doubt, and you will be unshakable yet open to whatever confronts you. If you don't have faith in Hanmaum Juingong, no matter how well you are able to do things there is still an unseen fifty percent that you haven't taken care of. When the root is healthy, the stalk will be sturdy, and when the stalk is sturdy, the seeds will ripen.

CHAPTER 6: GWAN(觀)[22] ENTRUST AND OBSERVE

ENTRUST AND LET GO OF EVERYTHING

The Wall of Fixed Ideas

"Letting go" means letting go of not only distressing and unpleasant things, but also every kind of fixed idea. We carry around so many fixed ideas such as "you" and "I," "good" and "bad." You made all of these fixed ideas, and as long as you cling to them, it's impossible for you to become one with your true nature, Juingong.

The worst prison in the world is the prison of thought. The most difficult wall in the world to overcome is the wall of fixed ideas. From a certain perspective, spiritual practice means freeing yourself from such prisons of thought. Thus, if you keep thinking "I'm just an unenlightened being," then because of that thought you cannot play any role other than that of an unenlightened being. Be very aware of the great difference a single thought can make.

Don't make a big deal about other people's level of spiritual development. If you discriminate between higher and lower, you will not be able to make progress in your own practice. Even though you truly know, do not give rise to the thought that you know. Even though you may be higher, do not think that you are higher. Even though someone else may be ignorant, you should not let yourself be caught by thoughts like that.

From the present viewpoint, something may clearly seem right or wrong. However, from the combined viewpoint of past, present, and future, things cannot so easily be called right or wrong.

You can roll a barrel only when you are outside of the barrel. When you are caught by fixed ideas, it is as if you are trapped inside of a barrel, so you cannot freely use your mind. If you escape from your fixed ideas, you will see that all of the thoughts and perspectives that you considered so precious are utterly ridiculous. Mind is formless and can freely go anywhere in the universe, so if you give rise to thoughts in a wise and all-embracing manner, you can escape from the barrel, from bondage, and from the prison that has no bars. How can you freely use your mind unless you first step outside of your own fixed ideas?

Fixed ideas are like a wisp of cloud or smoke, but nonetheless people find themselves blocked or captured by these. You would laugh if you saw someone tripped by a cloud, or if someone claimed that they were imprisoned by the air. But, in fact, people are endlessly being trapped by things no more substantial than air or clouds. They make a wall with their mind, and then it imprisons them. Inherently, there is no wall or anything to trip over. These things are mirages they've created from the thoughts they gave rise to.

Do not insist upon your own fixed ideas. Your persistence is your own narrow mind. If your mind is broad, it can easily embrace the entire world. However, if your mind is narrow, even a needle cannot enter. You have to keep letting go of your stubbornness, and always be deeply respectful of all life and things. This is returning to and relying upon the Buddha-Dharma. This is also how to become a free person. Always be humble. Be humble. The fragrance of your broad and generous mind will warm other's hearts.

Thoughts of "I"

Clinging to the idea that you and others are different, to the extent that you cannot even imagine "everything is just one," is the fundamental obstacle that blocks the path to Buddha. At first, focusing on "I" may seem somewhat helpful, but, in fact, it is the foundation of evil. Clinging to these thoughts of "I" actually prevents us from being able to participate in the Buddha realm, and prevents us from experiencing the incredible benefits of that participation. Until we thoroughly know the truth of non-duality, there can be no lasting peace for us. Therefore, as a practitioner you must not view anything dualistically, and you must heavily and sincerely release everything into your foundation and go forward.

Wisdom is knowing that "I" does not exist. Wisdom is knowing that matter and the physical body are merely images in a dream, that they are just drops of water stirred up by the wind and waves. Ignorance is nothing other than insisting that an individual "I" exists, while forgetting that the physical body and matter cannot avoid disappearing. Just throw away "I", and a million kinds of suffering and confusion will all fall asleep. "My possessions, my thoughts, my fame, what I deserve," all of these imprison you inside of a barrel. Unfortunately, unenlightened people usually think that these are defensive walls that can protect them when they face troubles and difficulties. Therefore, you try to make them higher and thicker as time goes on. However, as you do this, your mind shrinks and becomes cold. As a result, this wall is not something that protects you, it is a wall that hurts you, a wall that imprisons you.

Nothing can be put in a bowl that is completely full. You cannot put anything into a mind that is already filled with thoughts of "I," attachments, desires, and the self-pride that insists that you are the best. A bowl has to be emptied before it can benefit from new things. When your stomach is empty, you can enjoy food. However, if your stomach is full, then even though a sumptuous feast is before you, you can't take even one bite. One of the truths of life is that once you let go of everything, you gain everything.

You should be able to find the egotistic pride that is subtly hidden within your mind. This kind of honesty and wisdom is essential. As you keep practicing, the layers of "me" will peel away one by one, and the wall that separates all lives will gradually disappear. The person who sees everything equally never falls into egotistic pride, and is on the path that becomes wider and wider.

> All sages
> since time immemorial,
> have shown that "I" does not exist.
> Nevertheless,
> people cling to "I"
> and wander around for the whole day.
> Suddenly the sun sets,
> and it's time to go to bed.

Clinging and Habits, Defilements[23] and Delusions

Nothing is yours. Be free from all ideas of having. If things can be said to belong anywhere, they belong to the foundation. You are merely managing the things that come into your life. Take care of those people and things as best you can, but be free from any ideas of possessing them.

Even if you move your belongings from this room to that room, those things are still yours. If the whole world is your house, what does it matter if something is in this room or that room? "Having" is just moving things from one room to another. This is how awakened people use their minds. Thus, when they need something, it comes to them naturally. Because they don't have the thought of "mine," they freely roam the universe, one with everything.

Don't cling to your body. If you are too attached to it, you'll have a hard time leaving it behind when the time comes. Thus, at the end of their lives, many people spend years in pain. It's like shelling peas. It's hard to do when the pod and peas are all stuck together. However, if the peas are ripe, the shell easily falls away. Likewise, if you are not attached to your body, you can freely leave when it's time.

As the sea and the waves are not separate, enlightenment and deluded thoughts are not two. So don't spend your time trying to figure out which thoughts are deluded and which are not— just let go of everything. When you do this, thoughts of "I," discriminations, and deluded thoughts will naturally disappear.

When thoughts arise, do not think of them as deluded thoughts, and never try to cut them off. The idea of trying to get rid of them is itself a deluded thought. The fact that thoughts arise is not the problem. After all, if thoughts didn't arise, it would mean you were a corpse, not a living person! In order to be free from deluded thoughts, you have to first free yourself from your fixed ideas about what is deluded. The way to free yourself is to just entrust everything to Juingong, instead of trying to figure out, "What kind of thought is this?"

Because even deluded thoughts arise from Juingong, entrust everything to Juingong, completely let go of it. When you return defilements and delusions inside, to your fundamental mind, its evolutionary power can shine forth.

Lotus flowers bloom in mud, and the Buddha-Dharma blooms in the midst of defilements.

I've never said that you shouldn't possess money, fall in love, or be upset when angry. Do all of this as you need to. But it is important to know that all of this is being done by your foundation. Watch and see if you are doing things from attachments to "I" or "mine." If you live harmoniously, knowing that there is nothing that is not yourself, you will be able to take everything in the world as material for your spiritual practice. If you are truly able to live like this, your every thought and word will manifest in the physical world. At this stage, you will understand the meaning of "the all-reaching hands and feet of Buddha."

Questioning

While entrusting everything to Juingong, sometimes questions will suddenly arise within you. "Why did things turn out like this?" "What's the fundamental principle behind these things?" "How can I have sensation and perceptions if all things are truly not separate?" "Why is it said that all things are empty?" "I'm doing all kinds of things, so why is it said that Juingong is the one that is doing everything?" All kinds of questions will arise.

If you go forward while relying upon only Juingong, then questions will arise naturally. This is true questioning and great questioning. This kind of questioning arises like fresh spring water. Trying to intentionally make up questions is like rotating empty millstones—nothing is produced and you just wear yourself out. Intentionally made questions and naturally arising questions are as different as heaven and earth.

If you try to make up questions using your intellect, these won't be true questions nor will any true answers arise. When you wholeheartedly believe in and entrust everything to your foundation, questioning bursts forth. When you let go again of even these questions, the answers will arise from within.

When questions naturally arise, if you do not know the answer, just let go of the question and go forward. Eventually the answer will come out. When you entrust questions to your foundation like this, it naturally takes care of them. Sometimes I use the word "peaceful" to describe this. But this doesn't mean

"I feel peaceful because I have let go, because deluded thoughts have been cut off." At true self, the foundation, everything functions together without any hindrance, and is always changing and flowing, so that when something is entrusted there, an appropriate response naturally arises. This is why I use the word peaceful.

Great questioning[24] gives birth to great enlightenment. Great questions naturally appear from inside after you can absolutely entrust all obstacles to your foundation and after true self is revealed. These questions are not intentionally made; they arise naturally. Great questioning is the best kind of questioning: it is given by true self in order to teach you. Furthermore, if you let go of even those questions and go forward, the answer will suddenly occur to you, either immediately or sometimes later when the time is right.

HOW TO LET GO
Faith and Letting Go
Letting go is itself belief. Without faith, you can't let go. You need to completely let go of everything, knowing that Juingong is taking care of it all, no matter whether things seem to be going well or badly. How can you completely let go if you do not believe?

How should you entrust everything to your inherent nature? First, sincerely believe in your inherent nature, Juingong, and know that it is taking care of everything. Second, go forward with courage. Third, experiment with how Juingong takes care of everything, continuously apply what you experience, and never let yourself be daunted by anything.

Letting go is not saying, "I don't care" or living in denial. If you try to let go with the attitude that "I don't care," or "Please make things go well," while hoping for a miracle without any effort on your own part, then this is not truly letting go. When you act like this, you're treating Juingong, your foundation, as if it were something separate from yourself. When you let go, you let go single-mindedly, knowing your foundation is the only thing that can truly take care of everything. Let go knowing that everything arises from Juingong, so only Juingong is able to solve everything.

Let Go Unconditionally

There are no justifications or reasons involved in letting go. As soon as something arises, unconditionally entrust it to Juingong, your foundation. Entrust everything to Juingong: entrust the things you understand and the things you don't understand, entrust happiness and entrust suffering, entrust poverty and entrust disease. Let go of things that are not going well, and let go of things that are going well. Let go, knowing "Only Juingong can truly show me the path." By letting go like this, you can empty your mind and unload the heavy luggage you have been carrying for eons. By letting go like this, you can clean up the dust of your mind, which has been accumulating for eons, and you can truly live and truly die.

Don't try to take care of things by relying upon theories, sutras, clever words, or other people's ideas. Instead, just let go while believing that only Juingong can solve it. Let go once, let go twice, let go continuously, so that you are used to letting go. Keep letting go, so that it becomes second nature, like taking off your shoes when you enter a house. Then even problems of genetics and karma will melt down.

Let Go to Emptiness

Where should we let go to? Let go to emptiness. What is emptiness? Emptiness means all lives changing and manifesting every instant, and functioning together as one. Every single thing is empty, including myself. Everything is part of this emptiness, everything is subject to the law of emptiness. Everything is changing and manifesting, including myself, so we are inherently living while letting go. Even the thought "I've done…," has no place to stick to. Thus there's no need to even say "let go" or "entrust." However, many people don't understand this, so I say "let go to emptiness" as a method to help them realize the truth. How could we live without letting go to emptiness?

Karma is the absolutely unavoidable result of what we have done. It arises continuously from within us. I'm concerned that if I say to just let go of everything, it may seem too ambiguous or cause some people to fall into nihilism. So I have said, "Take emptiness as the central pillar, and let go of everything to that." When a pinwheel rotates, it relies upon its central point. Likewise, you have to make Juingong your foundation, your center point. Rely upon this center and entrust it with all things. When you can do this, you can live with vitality and you can live freely, like flowing water.

All things are directly connected to each other through the foundation, and unseen energy flows back and forth between all lives and things. However, when people discriminate, clinging to some things and rejecting or avoiding others, they block this energy from flowing freely. Thus if you just let go and entrust everything to your foundation, to Juingong, this energy can flow naturally, exactly as needed.

Although it is said that you should let go inwardly or return things inward, in fact Juingong is neither inside nor outside. Juingong is the combination of all things in the universe, and existed before all of those things. Although it cannot be grasped, it can be grasped.

THE VIRTUE AND MERIT OF LETTING GO
When you keep letting go of everything to Juingong and observing, karma will collapse, habits will melt down, your true

self will be revealed, and every kind of hindrance will surrender to you. Juingong is like a mailbox. If you put something into Juingong and observe, it will be delivered and a reply will return.

When people hear "Let go of everything," they often ask, "How can I live if I do that?" However, when you let go, you can truly live. Unenlightened people believe that it is necessary to plan and think carefully about every single thing. However, awakened people don't raise thoughts for each little thing they do. Instead, they just rest deeply. Yet everything they do is in accord with the Dharma, without even the slightest error. Because they let go, their actions are more harmonious, natural, profound, sincere, beautiful, and more beneficial than any actions that are done by relying on intellect or planning. Thus for a true practitioner, everything in daily life is itself the path. Because they let go and rest, every single thing they do, whether moving, standing, sitting, or lying down, is all naturally in accord with the Dharma.

If you try to practice by depending upon some specific regimen or physical method, in the beginning your goal may seem clear and close at hand. However, as you go further, your path becomes hazy and eventually it will come to a dead end. On the other hand, if you keep letting go and entrusting, and experiencing the results of this, then the path that seemed narrow in the beginning will gradually widen, and in the end will become a great avenue and gateway to the truth.

Living while completely letting go of everything produces infinite virtue and merit. First, every kind of suffering will collapse. Second, habits that have been sustained for eons by karmic affinity will all melt down. Third, the defilements and delusions that filled the mind will gradually disappear, and eventually there will be nothing to be empty and nothing to be full. At this point, your true self will be clearly revealed.

Spiritual practice is like building a house—when you have reached this point, you have a strong foundation, and are therefore ready to begin erecting the pillars that will support what comes next.

UNCEASING PRACTICE

The Correct Attitude for Practicing

You must not try to search outside of yourself. Take your inherent nature as your teacher. Because your inherent nature exists, everything in the universe functions together, so take your inherent nature, your fundamental mind, as your teacher.

In this practice, you teach yourself and you learn from yourself. You let go and you receive. You surrender and you accept the surrender. Spiritual cultivation is done like this, between you and your true self. Don't be caught by outside things.

God, Buddha, and Avalokiteshvara Bodhisattva all exist within you. If you would find and know them, start by brightening your own inner light. Then you will also be able to correctly perceive yourself and the world around you. However, if you abandon your own inner light and search for Buddha or God outside yourself, you will not find them, and little you do will turn out well.

Flowers bloom naturally when the conditions are right. People should learn about the conditions that cause flowers to bloom, and then create those conditions. Instead, they often wander around trying to find some unique and astonishing method. Instead of searching outside of yourself, you should first center your mind, and then take those thoughts that are focused on outward things and return them inward. Do not be dazzled by or chase after other people's enlightenment. Instead, create the conditions that will allow the flower of enlightenment that is within you to bloom. You're already endowed with it, so just help it to bloom naturally.

To a practitioner, tomorrow does not exist. Only here and now exists. You should not postpone things, assuming that somehow the situation will be better tomorrow. It won't be any different if you don't make an effort now. Today, here at this moment, you must see directly with clear eyes, and must go forward steadily and calmly, like the noble steps of an elephant moving through the forest. "Right here" is the place of the Buddha realm. "This moment" is the instant that Buddha is born, and is the instant that encompasses all of the past and future. Thus practitioners understand that this moment, this day, is all there is. This present moment is the instant of your birth, so it is in this moment that you must practice.

Go forward with steps that never leave any trace. Accept everything that confronts you with a positive attitude, and never try to avoid anything you face. It's not a problem of obtaining something, or getting rid of something, or not getting rid of something. Just make sure you aren't trying to avoid the things that are coming, and don't try to cling to the things that are leaving. Become a brave person who is never stained by anything or attached to anything. Become a true human being, a person who is both the most normal and the most extraordinary.

A courageous person covers a thousand miles with a single step; a small-minded person can run a hundred miles, and it still won't amount to even one step.

Practice is resting. If you want to awaken, then your mind should be calm and spacious. However, if you continuously give rise to the thought that you want to become a Buddha quickly or that you want to immediately escape the sufferings of an unenlightened being, then your mind will become narrower and more restless. The harder you try to grab something, the farther away it goes. Rest deeply, and it comes naturally. This is the magic of spiritual practice.

Practitioners must be honest with themselves. This is because your foundation is Buddha, and the nature of Buddha is emptiness, where no fixed ideas exist. No deceptions, excuses, or rationalizations can help you awaken to your foundation.

Accomplishing things naturally is the best way. Instead of using your intellect to make detailed plans in order to accomplish something, entrust it to your foundation. Your foundation is the source of all truth, so it is completely able to take care of whatever you entrust to it. Everyone can do this. Everyone can experience this. When you do experience this, you can open your eyes to the infinite ability within yourself, and you naturally feel deeply grateful for your foundation.

Never doubt that an ordinary unenlightened person like yourself is endowed with infinite ability. Giving up without even trying is the reason unenlightened people stay unenlightened.

Look at how water flows. When it meets a hole, it fills the hole and then continues flowing. When it meets a rock or hill, it flows around it and continues on. The practice of finding your true self should be done like this.

Practicing Meditation

How should you meditate? You can sit if you want to sit, stand if you want to stand, work if you want to work, or busily take care of your daily life—all of these can be practicing meditation. "Sitting" meditation means that you maintain a calm and steady mind while entrusting every single thing to Juingong, with the faith that Juingong is the source and destination of all things. Thus "sitting" meditation is possible in any circumstance—it is the mind that sits, not the body. As long as you let go and entrust with belief, your daily life itself can be meditation.

When some people first hear about letting go, it seems too ambiguous or difficult. They feel uncertain about what to do when they hear about letting go, because no method or detailed instruction is given. You may feel that you have to use sitting meditation in order to practice. However, your mind doesn't sit just because your body does. Meditation is done through mind, not through the body. You have to begin by taking care of problems through mind. You're doing things backward if you're trying to use your body to grasp your mind.

From the very beginning, you have to practice through mind. This mind should be your fundamental mind, not the false self, not "I." If you're trying to rely upon something other than mind, it's like trying to hold a shadow. Your basic direction is already wrong, so you can't avoid going astray. This is why I don't give people the traditional hwadus[25] to practice with.

Calm and steady practice, together with deep and sincere faith, is itself meditation. This can also be called true meditation, where you do not have even the thoughts "I'm doing...," or "I was sitting in meditation." It is also living meditation: you can practice in whatever circumstances you find yourself.

Light the lantern of your mind, and keep it bright every single day. Seon is nothing other than this. In your daily life, if you do not give rise to the illusion of "I," if you entrust everything to Juingong, and if your mind is completely unshakable, regardless of whether you find yourself in heaven or in hell, then this is true meditation.

Of course meditation can be practiced while sitting quietly in a peaceful place, but your daily life itself is also the place for practicing meditation. The twenty-four hours of your daily life can all be meditation. Even if you sometimes forget Juingong during the day, if you remember this fundamental power that moves and guides you, then at that instant all of the time you had forgotten about it disappears, and it's as if there were never a break in your practice.

There are many methods with the goal of spiritual awakening, but if you do not practice through mind, ultimately all of those methods will be useless. Once you truly understand how to practice through mind, you can practice yoga, contemplation, or sitting meditation as you wish. Spiritual cultivation does not depend upon any style or routine of practice.

Hwadu

Daily life itself is a hwadu, so there is no need to receive a hwadu from others or to give a hwadu to others. Your very existence is a hwadu. Thus, if you are continuously holding on to a hwadu someone else gave you, when will you be able to solve your original hwadus? Trying to solve another person's hwadu is like turning empty millstones or spinning a car's wheels without moving forward.

Your body itself is a hwadu. Birth itself is a hwadu. Work itself is a hwadu. The vast universe is a hwadu. If you want to add more hwadus to these, when will you be able to taste this infinitely deep world we live in?

Are you going to block what is inherently open and then ask, "What is it?" For example, when you clearly understand that you are looking at a soda bottle, what benefit do you expect to get by asking "What is this?" Let go of the things you know and move on. Hwadus are merely an example of skillful means. If you ask about what you already know, saying "What is this?" you'll just make yourself confused. If you go forward while letting go, then what you really do not know will arise as questions from the invisible and non-material realm. You have to practice with what's confronting you right now. The seed has already germinated and is growing into a tall tree. What could you hope to gain by ignoring your own tree and searching for the seed of someone else's tree?

You have to completely entrust even a hwadu to your foundation, and let it work naturally. Changing, manifesting, and working together is the law of reality. So you need to live in accordance with this truth and entrust even hwadus to your foundation. However, some people cling so tightly to hwadus that they are unable to let go of them, and so cannot taste the truth. If you receive the hwadu "What is this?" you have to completely entrust it to your foundation, and let your foundation solve it. If you use your intellect to play with ideas and concepts, the hwadu won't be of any help to you whatsoever.

GWAN (OBSERVING)

As things confront you, let them go to your foundation and continue to observe. Even if the sky collapses, continue to let go and observe. Let go of everything to your foundation and watch, because everything functions together as one through your foundation. Although I tell you to observe and entrust to your foundation all of the things and difficulties that confront you, fundamentally none of those things are separate from Hanmaum. Nonetheless, you still need to keep observing and entrusting them. If you keep practicing like this, your focus will change from letting go and observing to trying to find the foundation, the true self that watches you let go and observe.

Observing means watching the center that has no fixed shape and never stands still. Observing is not praying for something. Begging Juingong for help is praying, not entrusting and observing. Just have faith in Juingong and entrust it with everything. And keep watching. Input everything to the computer that is the mind and pay attention to what comes out. Connect with your inherent Buddha and observe how the things you entrusted are taken care of naturally and automatically. What benefit do you think you will obtain by ignoring your own inherent Buddha and begging others for help?

Keep watching. Keep watching your own steps. Keep watching who is talking, who is listening and who is seeing. Keep watching the one that has been doing everything in your daily life. If you are looking for truth in some place other than your daily life, you will never find it. Carefully observe your tears, laughter, suffering, and happiness. Right there, do the things you cry and laugh about truly exist? Does the self who cries and laughs truly exist? Keep watching very closely and carefully.

Even if you're facing an emergency that seems beyond your ability, entrust that to Juingong and keep watching. Have faith in Juingong, and continue to entrust and observe. Keep watching without discriminating between things. Juingong, your foundation, will take care of whatever you entrust it with. Firmly believe this and go forward. This is meditation, this is entrusting and observing. Have faith in Juingong and keep entrusting it with whatever confronts you, and just keep watching what comes out. Don't beg for the outcome that is most appealing to your own fixed ideas. Although the things you have created over countless eons steadily come out, if you let go as they confront you, then what has been input will be erased. Keep watching this process.

When you entrust things to Juingong, never think of yourself and Juingong as being separate. Inherently, you and Juingong are one. You are the one who lets go, and at the same time you are also the one who receives. Likewise, there is no separation between the one who is watching and what is being watched. If you are distinguishing between the one who is watching and what is watched, then this is not true entrusting and observing.

THE PATH TO AWAKENING

Enlightenment does not mean getting rid of an unenlightened self, and then finding a self that is a Buddha somewhere else. Because you are a Buddha, there is no self to throw away, and no self to find. Just get rid of ignorance and delusions, and you will know that you are a Buddha and that you are already complete as you are. If you awaken to this, you will burst out laughing at how much effort you spent in order for you to become yourself. This is the laughter of peace and joy.

Enlightenment means never being stained by living and dying, even though you live in the world of creation and disappearance. It is knowing that you do not throw away this realm and go to another realm. It is knowing that enlightenment exists in the midst of defilements, instead of thinking that you have to throw away defilements in order to reach a separate state of enlightenment. Enlightenment is knowing that there is no absolute self that exists apart from the self that has defilements, delusions, and worries right now. It is knowing that thinking, hearing, and false thoughts all arise from Hanmaum. All of these are enlightenment.

If you pay attention only to emptiness and ignore the material world, or if you ignore your present circumstances, saying "Everything is impermanent," or "There is no self," then this is not the middle way. If you see only one side but not the other side, then you have deviated from the middle way, without which there is no enlightenment.

In order to thoroughly understand yourself and reach enlightenment, you must die three times, and these three times are also not three times. After dying the first time, you find yourself. After dying the second time, you know that all things are not two. And, after dying the third time, you are able to manifest non-dually. That is to say, you must overcome three stages that are not fixed stages: First, return all things and obstacles to your foundation. If you keep doing this, you will eventually discover your fundamental nature. Then, once you discover your true self, you have to let go of even this with mindless mind. If you keep doing this, you'll truly realize that you and all existence are not separate. Finally, if you keep letting go like this, even mindless mind will melt down, and the state of true emptiness will be reached. At this point, you are able to manifest non-dually. Although the stages are different, the way you have to practice is the same for each: return inwardly, see all things as yourself—never as something separate—and let go of even this and go forward.

If you're a practitioner with firm belief, there are no stages in spiritual practice, because the truth, in its entirety, is functioning equally at every single place and time; thus it is accessible to every single one of us, at every instant. In this sense there are no stages, but from another point of view stages clearly exist. You must pass through them and go forward without being lazy.

SEEING YOUR INHERENT NATURE
The first stage of practice, letting go of the self that is an unenlightened being, lasts until you know your true self. At this stage, a practitioner "dies" for the first time and, at the same time, is newly born.

At this first stage, a practitioner needs to return attention to Juingong, and gather all of the thoughts that are going outward, and entrust them all to Juingong together with all the obstacles and everything else that arises. At this stage belief is the most important thing. It must be extremely sincere. You also need courage, so that at every moment you can let go of the mind that is caught by various things and circumstances. You need courage because when you let go like this, what you have thought of as yourself dies.

This stage is the practice of breaking up the illusion of the false self, which has been created through your own discriminatory thinking. If you can consistently practice like this, then it can be said that you are truly practicing seon. If the practice of throwing away the false self deepens and becomes extremely genuine, then while in the midst of this *samadhi*26 true nature naturally appears. It is like the baby being born after the pregnancy. From the viewpoint of the self that is an unenlightened being, this practice is like dying because you're entrusting all things that confront you and you're letting go of all attachments. However, from the viewpoint of Juingong, this is the process of being born.

When true nature appears, you will feel indescribable happiness. But this is not the end. From this point, you must go forward from the perspective of your foundation, the true doer. This is when true practice begins.

Even if you have found yourself and have become one with your true self, you must still continue to practice and go forward. This is an extremely difficult period of time. Because you know true self and are not caught by anything, you can become very comfortable. Thus it's easy for you to stay at that stage, thinking, "This is it!" You'll be very happy and comfortable; it is as if you are drinking the sweet spring water of life, which you hadn't even dreamed of when you were wandering around inside of suffering. So it will feel like you've achieved a lot, and it will be difficult to even imagine that there might be higher levels of practice. You won't think about these higher levels because you have never seen or heard about them. Moreover, when you look around, you'll see all kinds of people who are at levels of existence lower than your own, so it will be easy for you to think that you are the best. Everything above is dark and only below is clear. You have to realize what a vulnerable stage this is. If you're not careful, it's very easy to go astray.

It is very difficult to become perfectly enlightened all at once. Why? Because you've created so many habits, over countless lives, that it's extremely hard to drop all of them at once. There-fore, don't think that you have to let go of everything all at once; instead just keep letting go of things as they arise. By doing this, you can have experiences and deepen your prac-tice. As you entrust those things to Juingong, that karma melts down and those habits fall away. As you let go and let go, you also grow up. And even when you suddenly awaken, don't make a big deal about it. You must die again, without remaining sep-arate from anything that confronts you.

BECOMING A BUDDHA

At the stage of "dying" a second time, a practitioner begins to have mysterious abilities. However, these are one of the things you have to let go of and throw away. If any of *the five subtle pow-ers*[27] arise, then, as they occur, just let go of them to your foun-dation and go forward. Because you let go with mindless mind of whatever comes, your situation is different from other people who may have subtle abilities. There are some people with these abilities, but it is often the case that they don't know the principle of non-duality and are not used to letting go to the foundation, so they think to themselves, "These powers are such a wonderful treasure." If someone continues clinging to and trying to increase these powers, then not only are they wasting time on a path that cannot lead to freedom, but there is also a great risk that they will end up going insane.

If you understand that ultimately all things have arisen from your mind, and if you return and entrust even the subtle powers to your inherent mind, then mindless mind will be achieved. It is called mindless mind because mind is naturally undisturbed. If this stage of mindless mind deepens, questions such as "Does the self exist or not?" do not arise. At this stage, who you are is so different from the "I" that unenlightened people usually think of as themselves that it could be correctly said that "I" doesn't exist. On the other hand, there is the one that actually lives in the world, so it is also correct, from another perspective, to say that "I" exists. In other words, mindless mind is a completely empty state where even the thought of mindless mind is naturally let go of—not a state where there is nothing, but a perfectly empty state that is able to do or become anything. It is the emptiness that can dissolve all suffering and ignorance, and where even mindless mind dissolves.

NIRVANA

You must "die" one more time after "dying" twice. In addition, you must keep it a secret. When you reach this stage, although there is clearly "you" and "I," you can become me, and I can become you, without either being "you" or "me." At this stage, you come to understand the powerful principle of manifestation. You can manifest like this because mind inherently has no form, so it can appear in an infinite number of different shapes.

After you thoroughly "die" for the third time, the stage of manifestation opens up. There are many mysterious things about this stage of manifestation. The story from the Vimalakirti-nirdesa Sutra where the Buddha gathered together five hundred parasols and made them into one is not a myth, it is true. It is also true that the parasol showed everything in the

Buddha realm. At this stage, if you sit peacefully, you are a Buddha. If you give rise to a thought, you become a Bodhisattva, and can take care of unenlightened beings throughout all realms. There is just no way words can describe everything about this stage.

Thus, freeing yourself alone from the cycle of suffering, birth, and death is not the final stage of one's practice. Through the mysterious and profound truth that is the Buddha-Dharma, you can hear the needs of all unenlightened beings and you can save all unenlightened beings. You can do all of this with hands that are not hands and feet that are not feet. All of this is possible because through the power of the Buddha-Dharma anything can be done, even in the material world. That is to say, all laws of the material world are encompassed and governed by the Buddha-Dharma. The great meaning of the Buddha-Dharma is so vast and complete that it is almost beyond comprehension.

True Nirvana is attained while you are alive, not after you are dead. Further, when you let go and throw away even the thought that you have reached Nirvana, then this is complete Nirvana. When you reach complete Nirvana, you will know how to come back to the Nirvana of existence. You must thoroughly experience the level where there is no bone, no flesh, where there is nothing.

THE MIDDLE PATH

When you're able to treat the realms of enlightenment and non-enlightenment equally and harmoniously, this is following the middle path.

There is no need to think that one side is meaningless and one side is precious. Let go of both sides. There is no need to accept one side and reject the other. The impulse to accept or reject arises from your own fixed thoughts. Encompass both sides; treat them equally. It is not the left foot, it is not the right foot. It is both feet together, just as they are.

There's no need to keep one thing and throw away something else. You need to be able to take care of both at the same time. It is not a matter of choosing one or the other. You should not lose yourself in emptiness, and you should not lose yourself in the material. You must combine the fifty percent that is the visible realm with the fifty percent that is the unseen realm.

The middle way means the great emptiness, the whole that encompasses all extremes.

THE VIRTUE AND MERIT OF AWAKENING

If you truly awaken to the fundamental nature of mind, you will be free and at ease, and will no longer be a slave to the cycle of karma and rebirth. You're free because you're not disturbed by anything that arises from inside or outside. The fixed concept of "I" has melted away. You manifest as a doctor or a nurse, as a judge, a prosecutor, or a lawyer. You manifest as a president, a farmer, or a prostitute. Through your fundamental mind, you manifest as anything that is needed. You manifest in millions of ways, without limitation, and take care of all visible and invisible things without any hindrances—that is the ability of a truly free person.

If you awaken, then because the truth of all existence is within your fundamental mind, there is nothing that is not an entrance, nothing that is not a poem, nothing that is not Dharma, and nothing that is not a treasure.

If one person awakens, uncountable seeds of that awakening will spread all over the world. Although it is difficult, if one person becomes enlightened, uncountable numbers of seeds that support and guide all beings will spread throughout this world, as well as other realms.

PART THREE:
APPLYING THE PRINCIPLE OF ONE MIND

CHAPTER 8: THE ESSENCE OF BUDDHISM LIES IN APPLYING AND EXPERIENCING

Even though the truth that Shakyamuni Buddha taught is so vast and unlimited, if you don't experience it in your daily life, it's of no more use than a picture of food to a hungry person. Even though you see it a hundred times, if you can't take hold of it and eat, it's useless. If you want to realize truth, the Buddha-Dharma, you have to experience it through your daily life, your body, and your mind. What could you possibly find by ignoring these and looking for the truth somewhere else? The Buddha taught people to experience the truth for themselves, because this is the only way to become truly free.

Even though you memorize all the names of the materials needed to build a house, such as bricks, plywood, beams, and roof tiles, if you don't actually put them together and build a house, they won't be much use, will they? The goal of the Buddha's teachings is application, not intellectual knowledge.

From the perspective of our fundamental mind, "just doing" is easier than speaking. Words may be inadequate or misunderstood, but doing is straightforward: if you do it, it's taken care of. However, people get caught by words, and argue about wrong and right without ever trying to experience the Dharma directly.

Don't get caught up in theories or arguments—just taste the truth for yourself. Instead of discussing whether the watermelon is ripe or not, just cut it open and take a bite. This is true meditation, and it is meditation in action. All visible and invisible phenomena are meditation in action. Thus as long as you think that enlightenment is something apart from your daily life, you will never realize enlightenment.

Study without action, and study not followed by practice, is merely accumulating lifeless knowledge. Doing once is better than seeing a hundred times. True wisdom is obtained only through applying and experiencing.

Although perhaps you have been a practicing Buddhist for decades, if you cannot take a drink of clear spring water, and cannot give that water to others, then when can you pay back your debts, and when can you give light and wisdom to others? Although you have the potential to become a Buddha, unless you put what you have learned into practice, you cannot rise above the level of an unenlightened being.

CHAPTER 9: PRACTICE IN DAILY LIFE

LIFE ITSELF IS DHARMA

The Buddha-Dharma is the fruit that has ten thousand flavors, the flower with ten thousand fragrances. It can be said that practitioners are the farmers who raise these fruits and the gardeners who tend these flowers. Practicing the Buddha-Dharma is the most rewarding and most beneficial kind of farming. Furthermore, you don't need to disregard the other things in your daily life in order to do this. You can do the farming of the Buddha-Dharma while working at your regular job, because your livelihood provides the experiences that will help you deepen your practice of the Buddha-Dharma.

The Buddha-Dharma is the law of reality and the law of daily life. If you can truly bring your thoughts and actions into accord with what the Buddha taught, then you will awaken to the profound truth, with which you can solve any problems, not only those of individuals, but also the problems of societies and nations. Neither religion nor spiritual awakening exists apart from your daily life.

The Buddha-Dharma encompasses all of the things you do in your life—walking, speaking, and moving. Thus the truth taught by every Buddha exists not only in the Dharma Hall, but also in your bedroom, kitchen, and workplace. The lives of laypeople and teachers are not different in terms of practice.

You must practice the Buddha-Dharma while adapting to your own situation. Do not think about trying to jump out of it or about throwing something away. Instead, just keep going forward diligently in the midst of your own life and circumstances, with your mind leading your body and your body leading your mind.

HANDLING DIFFICULTIES AND SUFFERING

Even if somebody is causing you great hardship, never see that person as being separate from yourself. Don't distinguish between "me" and "others." Don't be blinded by beautiful appearances, and don't be awed by great things. Because you exist, they also exist. Because you exist, all kinds of difficulties are able to arise. Because all things in the universe are working as one, as Hanmaum, all other people are also fundamentally yourself. Never be shaken. No matter whether you meet Buddha, or the King of Demons, or a Dharma-protecting spirit, everything is merely another shape of yourself.

When you face hardships, don't become depressed, asking yourself "Why do such difficulties happen to me?" When these things happen, you should think "Now I have an opportunity to grow up." Your future depends upon which way you choose. You have been given the authority to decide your future.

Bad circumstances are, in fact, an opportunity to learn. When you understand that those things are Juingong teaching you, you cannot help but be thankful for even those circumstances. In fact, when difficulties come, you can make more progress in your practice. Thus, your practice deepens and you gain wisdom and strength.

"Quietly embrace your difficulties" does not mean to just endure them. It means knowing that the difficulties you face are inherently empty, and furthermore, that those difficulties can guide and train you. This is the attitude of practitioners who quietly embrace all things.

Dreaming is being awake, and being awake is a dream. Do not look upon dreams and your waking hours as separate. If you think that dreams and your waking hours are different, you cannot know the deeper place.

When you are aware that you're dreaming, you're not bothered by the things that happen in the dream. Likewise, those people who understand that defilements are also nothing other than a kind of dream are never deceived by those things. Even in a dream, don't see things as separate from yourself, and don't allow yourself to get caught up in the things that happen.

People try to escape from suffering, but they do not try to understand the true causes of suffering. Thus, although they can get away from one instance of suffering, they cannot avoid having to face more suffering in the future. The thought of "I" is like a factory that continuously produces suffering and joy. You are the one who has made these things, so you are the only one who can solve them. In order to do this, don't think of these things as fate or karma, just entrust all suffering and everything that confronts you to your true self and keep watching and letting go.

If you look at who you are now and what kind of person you are, it's possible to see how you lived in the past. If you look at what you are doing now, you can see what your life will be like in the future. When the winds and rains come, all of the dust and pollution is cleaned away. Although it may not seem like it at the time, later you will realize that the suffering you are experiencing is actually Buddhas and Bodhisattvas who have come to purify you and help you grow.

ILLNESS

When something goes wrong with your body it's often necessary to go to a drugstore or a doctor, but you need to first remember your fundamental mind. It connects everything and is where everything starts, so entrust that condition to it. And while you're being treated, keep entrusting that situation to your foundation. Further, if you remember that the doctor and you are connected as one through your foundation, and entrust this thought to your foundation, then the treatment tends to be much more successful.

As with most problems, there is a portion that others can help you with, but only you can take care of the most fundamental parts. You do this by entrusting everything, even disease and pain, to your foundation. This is because everything, including disease, arises from your foundation, so that is where the solutions also need to start from.

Disorders with the body often happen when the lives that make up our bodies don't view things from the perspective of the whole body. They don't know what's best for the whole and instead just fight among each other, seeking advantage and domination. Thus, one way of curing disease is to teach all of those lives that fundamentally they are living and working together as one life: what happens to one affects the whole.

Entrust to our foundation the thought that we are all sharing the same life, the same mind, the same body, working together as one, and freely give and receive whatever is needed, then through our foundation that thought is instantly communicated to all the lives in our body. When the lives within our body can coexist harmoniously, when they know that other lives are also their life, then a multitude of problems with our bodies will improve or even disappear. It's often possible to live a normal life even though something like cancer doesn't disappear because those cells are now living harmoniously with the rest of the lives that make up the body.

Other people's Buddha-nature and your Buddha-nature are

the same. All people and lives are connected as one through this foundation. So when we entrust to our foundation a thought or intention for someone, that energy is communicated. Even if someone doesn't know anything about spiritual practice, nonetheless, that energy is still communicated and felt at a very deep level.

As with nearly all problems, there is still a portion that people must solve themselves. However, imagine the case where someone has to do a job in a cold and dark setting. Now imagine someone doing the same job in a warm and bright atmosphere, with healthy food and warm clothes. Which case is likely to turn out better? Which is likely to go smoother? This is why, and how, we can help others through our fundamental mind.

MONEY AND PROSPERITY

Spiritual practice is wisely taking care of the things that confront you in your daily life—including even issues of money and property. So no matter whether you have a little money or a lot, understand that you only *manage* it, you don't own it. In fact, that money has no owner, it is not your money, it is not other's money—it is something that is endlessly circulating. It comes and it goes. So continuously let go of your attachments to it.

When someone earns money, they often think that they alone earned that money. But, without other's help, it wouldn't have been possible to earn even a single penny. In one sense, it's easy to see that money is earned with the help of employees, customers, employers, and so forth. However, beyond even this, from the perspective of the foundation, all beings worked together to earn that money. So that money can't be said to belong to you alone.

Profit and loss are like the front and back sides of a coin: they always work as a pair, never alone. You have to know this. When you have a profit, don't get caught up in that, and when you have a loss, don't become despondent about it. Although many people cry and laugh because of profits and losses, if you can stay focused on your fundamental mind, you'll feel more at ease and be less likely to lose your way when wonderful or terrible things happen in your life.

With all things, know your own means and live within them. Do not cling to things; instead, live harmoniously, knowing that there is nothing that is not you.

FAMILY

The path of becoming a Buddha lies in the midst of taking care of your family and looking after the people in your life. Take the things that confront you right now and melt them down. If you talk and worry about things that are far away, while ignoring the tasks that are right in front of you, this can be called the mind of greed. If you cannot overcome the problems that face you in your daily life and home, then you are not at the stage where you can talk about the Buddha-Dharma. You must throw away everything without throwing away anything. This means that you throw away attachments, but you do not throw away the people and situations that confront you in your life. Taking care of the things that arise in your life is the action of a Bodhisattva.

Do not cling to your children. Entrust your children to the energy of the foundation and live together harmoniously. When you live like this, without a doubt your children will eventually become Buddhas and Bodhisattvas.

If your spouse or children do bad things, never react to them with your mouth, body, or material things. Just entrust everything to the fundamental mind and observe. Just keep letting go of everything to your foundation. Then you can communicate with each other. If you dial a telephone on your side, the phone will ring on the other side. When you do this, your sincerity can be transmitted. This is truly loving them and is the expression of the Buddha-Dharma.

Before blaming your parents or children, your wife or husband, you need to know that all beings gather together according to their similar karma. You should also know that blaming others is one of the most spiritually harmful things you can do.

Not only does your state of mind and spiritual practice affect your child, but pregnancy is also a very powerful time to help your child's spiritual growth. Imagine a warm classroom filled with light, or always being surrounded by mature, wise friends. Think about the kind of influence this would have on your life and the choices you'd make. Like this, when you rely upon your foundation and entrust it with what confronts you, your child also experiences the energy and light of your foundation. Your unborn child is changing and growing so much that a small change or influence at this stage can have a great influence throughout the rest of his or her life. Furthermore, the thoughts the mother entrusts to her foundation have a much stronger influence then they normally would for someone else because, for those months, the mother and her unborn child are literally sharing the same physical body.

We tend to like people who treat us well, and dislike those who treat us badly. This even happens between married couples and between parents and children. We're happy when others say nice things to us, but when they sincerely point out our faults we often feel hurt or resentful. When we're happy with something or someone, we tend to like that thing or person even more. But when we don't like what they're saying, we may suddenly become angry. All of these behaviors harm us, so let go of them all to Juingong and always face things with a smile and kind words. If you can do this, true self, your inherent Buddha, silently helps all minds become harmonious.

TRUE LOVE

If a child falls into deep water, the parents just jump in and try to save him or her. They do it without any concern for whether they themselves die or not. They do it unconditionally. This love that instantly jumps into the water is the unconditional love of a parent and is also the unconditional love a Buddha has for all beings. The Buddha's love and compassion and parents' love and compassion for their children are both the same fundamental love. They all say, "I will save you, even if it takes everything I have." The true love of parents never expects to be paid back—this is compassion.

Even though others may seem better than you, don't look down upon yourself. Even though you may seem better than others, don't become full of yourself. Always try to be compassionate and broad-minded. Love each other, share each other's burdens, and share what you have with others. This kind of love is more than enough to take care of everything in the world.

Throw away stubbornness and arrogance. Let go of greed and desire, dissolve attachments and clinging, and free yourself from jealousy and envy. With a compassionate smile, entrust all of these harmful states of mind to your foundation, and let them melt down and become one. This is the love and action of a Bodhisattva. Anything else is not truly love or compassion; it is greed, attachment, and delusion.

HAPPINESS AND HARMONY

Joy and suffering arise at the point where you begin to discriminate between good and bad, between what you like and what you don't like. However, true happiness is more than the good feeling you get when things go your way. True happiness arises from letting go of your discriminations; it arises from the middle way, which transcends all dualities.

Happiness is something you make. Don't expect that someone else can give it to you. If you keep clinging to the idea that someone else is going to make you happy, every kind of suffering will follow.

People want their own life to go well, their family to be happy, and their nation to prosper. However, families quarrel, wars occur, and nations collapse. These kinds of things happen because people tend to act and think from a limited, incomplete perspective. If you can see all aspects of the things that confront you and can interact and function together as one with them, then all of those situations will be resolved harmoniously.

Even though you have to share a single piece of bread for a meal, it can be a happy time if you are all harmonious. Even though you have a sumptuous feast, if everyone is speaking harshly to each other, the meal won't be a pleasant experience. Where is hell? Who makes it? Even if you are very rich, and donate a lot of money and food to worthy causes, if your mind is narrow and full of greed, you won't be able to enjoy even the present moment, much less the good results of those donations. Mind is the source of everything, so saving yourself or not saving yourself depends upon how you use your mind. Whether you will be a poor person who is rich, or a rich person who is poor, all depends upon yourself. The Buddha's Pure Land does not exist in some far away realm. If you cultivate your mind, this world itself will naturally become the Pure Land.

CHAPTER 10: RELIGION AND DAILY LIFE

TEACHERS AND LEARNING THE PATH

For a blind person, a cane is necessary, and for a person with an injured leg, a crutch is necessary. Like this, for a practitioner a teacher is necessary. But good teachers can be hard to find. Be careful; don't abandon your own upright center and chase after others. If you follow a blind person, you'll fall into a ditch.

Once you have opened your eyes for yourself, once you have awakened to your true self, then you will be able to go forward taking that as your teacher. However, until then, it's valuable to follow a good teacher.

Taking refuge in the *Sangha*[28] does not mean blindly following sunims. What you should believe in is your own Buddha-nature, Juingong. Taking refuge in the Sangha means that when you think that the actions, words, and thoughts of a teacher all agree with each other, and don't go against your own conscience and good judgment, then you follow and accept that sunim as a teacher. In the process of practicing, you need not only an inner teacher but also an outer teacher, who can help you with your experiences. For example, *Huike*[31] was guided by Bodhidharma and *Wonhyo*[29] had *Daean*[30] for a teacher.

The resolute and unflinching mountains silently tell us, "Live like a mountain." The ceaselessly flowing waters whisper, "Live like water." The flowers that bloom in the midst of any kind of adversity quietly sing, "Live like a flower." A weed living in harsh soil says, "Live courageously." There is nothing that is not our teacher.

There is no place in the Buddha realm and universe that is not your place. No matter whether you are in the Dharma Hall or sitting on the toilet, because you exist at that place, true self exists together with you, and Buddha also exists together with you. Nevertheless, there are many people who ignore Juingong and wander around outside, trying to find a better teacher or a better place for praying. They don't know that within themselves they have their own Dharma Hall, which is always filled with light and where Buddha is always present.

BOWING

True bowing means keeping yourself humble and respecting Buddhas, Bodhisattvas, and sages. But at the same time, know that their mind and your mind are not two, and never lose your determination and resolution. Accordingly, even if you pray for the help of Buddhas and Bodhisattvas, you have to make the focus of that prayer within yourself. If your heart is extremely sincere, you may be able to have some experiences and achieve a certain amount of good fortune, but as long as you are searching outside of yourself, your efforts can never result in true virtue and merit. Nor will you achieve the great goal.

We bow to Buddha because Buddha's mind and our fundamental mind are not two. Also, bowing is surrendering your physical body and your thoughts of "I." Therefore, when bowing you should always try to be quiet, humble, and extremely sincere. And be grateful for everything.

Bowing reverently to Buddha and seon masters is bowing reverently to your true nature. Offering food to Buddhas and seon masters is offering food to Juingong. Indeed, the mind of Buddha, the mind of Bodhisattvas and Dharma-protecting spirits, the mind of patriarchs and seon masters of the past, and the mind of all ancestors and all unenlightened beings are together inside of Juingong, working as one. Therefore, bowing reverently and offering food with one mind is the same as bowing reverently and offering food together with all Buddhas and all unenlightened beings. Thus whether it's making an offering, or something else, you must not forget your foundation, Juingong.

In this modern era, when everybody is so busy trying to earn a living, how can you practice if you have to do one hundred and eight bows or three thousand bows a day? Mind is beyond time and space, does not have form, and is completely free, so one extremely sincere bow where you are one with your foundation can exceed bowing thirty thousand times.

If you bow once in front of Buddha, while returning everything to your foundation, your present mind, past mind, and future mind all function together as one mind, so one bow can surpass ten thousand bows. When you bow and put your forehead on the ground in front of Buddha, it means that Buddha's mind and your mind are not two, and that Buddha's body and your body are not two. Thus your flesh bows to your Juingong, your foundation.

Everything lives together as one and shares all things as one, so bow to your foundation, which makes this possible. Your foundation encompasses everything and connects it all as one, while transcending space and time; it is the functioning of your foundation that is the source of all laws and truths of the universe. Bow to the self that encompasses everything, not to the individual ego. When you give something or help others, do it from the foundation, not the individual "I." While bowing, know that everything is already combined with your foundation. True bowing is not directed outward; instead, it goes inward. Thus, if you truly bow to Buddha, you are bowing to Juingong, your foundation.

KEEPING THE PRECEPTS

The five precepts traditionally begin with "Do not...," but they can also be read positively. Thus, "Do not kill" becomes "Love all beings equally and compassionately." "Do not steal" becomes "Give alms and create virtue." "Do not engage in improper sexuality" becomes "Cultivate a pure and upright body and mind." "Do not lie" becomes "Speak only the truth and uphold trust." "Do not drink alcohol" becomes "Always maintain bright and upright wisdom." By understanding the precepts in this way, the precepts are not things you uphold by not doing something. Rather, you keep them by putting the Buddha's intention into action. When you rely upon and entrust everything to your inherently pure fundamental mind, all precepts are upheld naturally.

If it is dirty, clean it. If it is disorganized, straighten it up. If it is broken, fix it. This is keeping the precepts. Living sincerely and uprightly while taking care of the things in your life is keeping the precepts.

If you cultivate mind, you naturally uphold the precepts. People who fight with themselves, thinking "I must uphold the precepts," fail in the end to uphold the precepts. Regardless of whether it is the precepts or something else, you have to return everything to your foundation, then all precepts are naturally upheld. Nonetheless, practitioners should understand the history and intention behind the precepts. Understand them and entrust them to your foundation. In this way, you can apply them naturally in your daily life.

"Don't do this, don't do that" is not the true meaning of the precepts given by the Buddha. Even if something is good, if you overdo it, it can become bad. Although something is considered wrong, if you do it according to the needs and circumstances, it may not necessarily be bad.

If you let go of all things to your foundation, the precepts will be kept naturally, even though you don't constantly think about them. When this happens, precepts are the wings of freedom. Do not try to adapt yourself to the precepts. Rather, let the precepts, which are already within you, come out naturally.

If you completely let go of the thought of "I," and realize your inherent nature, the karma that you have piled up over eons cannot bind you. When you truly know your inherent nature, you also naturally know what the precepts are, so you won't have to try to distinguish between what is consistent with the precepts and what isn't.

But if you cling to formality and rules, your thoughts of "I" won't die and you won't be able to experience the spiritual realm. While keeping the precepts, you shouldn't be bound up by them. This is why the middle path is necessary. There's no need to go around creating disturbances. Love others. See all things equally, speak kindly and gently, and embrace others with a broad mind.

SUTRAS

The sutras are descriptions of how this world works. However, after the sutras appeared, some people spent all of their energy studying the sutras and so paid less attention to reality. Thus traditionally seon masters didn't allow disciples to read sutras at the beginning of their practice. If you get too caught up in the sutras, and cannot escape from them, all you'll ever achieve is becoming a bookworm.

Those people who read sutras but miss the true meaning are like bees that hit the window and die while trying to get to the flowers on the other side.

When you can firmly entrust everything to your foundation without being caught by anything, only then you can truly read sutras such as the Heart Sutra, the Diamond Sutra, the Lotus Sutra, or the Flower Ornament Sutra. If you correctly brighten your mind and clearly see yourself, only then you can refer to the teachings left by great teachers of the past. You have to know your true self; then, when you read sutras, you can under-stand the true meaning of the words. When you read sutras, don't see only the words; even if you don't read the sutras, you still have to know the fundamental truth they express.

Even though you have memorized the entire Diamond Sutra, if you haven't experienced the unseen half of reality, then you will only see and follow the words, not the Buddha's true mean-ing. Buddhism is *doing*. Buddhism is applying and putting into practice the truth of the sutras.

In the process of teaching people, all the Buddhas of history have used expressions and sayings that require deep reflection to understand. Don't treat these expressions carelessly: they con-tain great meaning. There are people who have only a superfi-cial understanding of these teachings and go around saying things like, "Everything is empty, so what is there to cling to?" But you shouldn't be so reckless. Only those people who have truly experienced the meaning of these expressions are free to talk about them. If someone who hasn't experienced it for him or herself just repeats these kinds of teachings, the karma from those actions won't disappear even after a million kalpas.

If people had correctly understood the truth, then past mas-ters wouldn't have needed to give so many methods and teach-ings. However, people didn't know the truth, so there had to be many Dharma talks and methods such as chanting, reading sutras, and lighting candles. Many places still follow those methods and traditions, but you must know the underlying meaning. Otherwise, you'll insist on using a horse cart in the age of the automobile. The important point is this: don't be dis-tracted by methods or traditions that were developed for past eras. Everyone needs to learn how to directly become a Buddha, instead of being burdened by all kinds of different methods.

RECITING THE BUDDHA'S NAME AND CHANTING SUTRAS

When those people who are one with their foundation chant sutras, the sound of their chanting permeates the entire universe and is heard by every Buddha and Bodhisattva. All things function together as one, so if you read sutras and chant mantras from this non-dual perspective, then true virtue and merit arises. However, if you don't know the deep meaning, your chanting doesn't reach the Dharma realm. You should know that when we recite the Heart Sutra or the Thousand Hands Sutra, we are learning the principles by which all visible and invisible phenomena function together as one, naturally and at every instant. If we put these principles into practice in our daily life, then we also learn how to go and come without going and coming.

Many Buddhists chant the name of Avalokiteshvara Bodhisattva, but in most cases, instead of brightening their own heart, they are looking for light from outside themselves. Because they're chanting with only their mouth, their hearts don't become brighter. If you don't know that your inherent nature is fundamentally bright, how can you save yourself and how can you give light to people around you?

Some people think that they must recite Buddha's name every day without fail. However, to those people who do not give rise to the thought of "I," a single thought can become reciting Buddha's name, a single thought guides the entire world, and a single thought becomes the manifestation of our true nature. You have to know this principle and not just chant the Buddha's name with only your mouth.

ONE WITH YOUR ANCESTORS

Your parents, ancestors, all Bodhisattvas, and all Dharma-protecting spirits exist within your mind. So in your daily life, if you earnestly entrust everything that confronts you to your fundamental mind, your life itself becomes a memorial service for your parents and an expression of gratitude to the Buddhas and ancestors.

Generally speaking, people assume that once someone is dead, there's nothing more that can be done for them. If we were separate, unconnected existences this would be true, but we are not such limited beings. While changing every instant, we are all connected as one by our fundamental nature, our Buddha-nature, our root. We are connected as one with all beings, whether they are in the next room or have left their body altogether.

Thus, we are able to give them light and energy according to our ability to become one with them. This means unconditionally entrusting everything about the situation to our foundation. It means completely letting go to our foundation of all of our worries, likes and dislikes, and the subtle habit of viewing things as fundamentally separate. We are a spiritual light for others to the extent that we can do this.

Often, people read a book or hear a talk and think they *know*. But they are wrong. They will truly know only through doing, through applying their understanding and experiencing for themselves. This first kind of "knowing" can even be considered a type of delusion and can be quite dangerous. Imagine someone who has only read a book about flying and thinks he knows all there is: What will happen to him when he has to finally get in the cockpit and take off?

Once people die, they can't, on their own, change their level of consciousness. It remains at the same level they experienced while alive. Furthermore, people sometimes get stuck at the level they were experiencing at the moment of death, which is unfortunately often a lower level than the level they lived their life at. When we become one with them, their consciousness is raised to our level, or to the level they lived their life at, if our level of consciousness is higher. Essentially, we're helping them become unstuck and move forward at a level that more accurately reflects the level they attained while alive.

Even a Buddha cannot raise the spirit of a deceased person higher than the level he or she had attained while alive. Thus, it is vital that we diligently cultivate our minds while alive and possessing a human body.

TRUE GIVING

If you view everything as your body, as your own pain, as your own situation, then how can your life be precious and someone else's life not be? This is true giving and the heart of a Bodhisattva.

Be able to forgive everything. When such a beautiful mind works together as one with all life and things in the universe, true giving—unconditional giving without "you" or "me"—will be possible.

When you give something, give it without any thought of giving. You should entrust even giving to Juingong and let go of it with deep sincerity. In a way, giving is like taking your money to a store and exchanging it for something else: even though you give something to others, you are not only giving it, you are also receiving it.

Try giving or helping others when you find yourself completely stuck. People often use so much energy worrying about what's "mine" that they actually end up blocking new things from coming to them. Everything is connected, and all energy inherently tries to flow among all things and lives equally, but our clinging and self-centered views end up blocking this energy.

Even though you gave a lot of help to others, if you did it with unpleasant thoughts or a grim face, then because there was some reluctance, it cannot become virtue and merit. Furthermore, no matter how many good actions you have done or how much you have donated, as long as you think "I did this...," it cannot become virtue and merit. Let go of the thoughts centered around "I" as soon as you become aware of them and go forward. When you see both the material and non-material as one, if you lift a single finger, it can move the entire universe. This virtue and merit is beyond comprehension.

Giving establishes the foundation with which you can repay your parents' kindness and can give sunlight to your children and strengthen their roots.

Giving can be compassion, and not giving can also be compassion; just make sure that it benefits others.

FATE AND DESTINY

When mind is bright, it is not because of fate. When mind is dark, it is not because of destiny. In the Buddha's Dharma, there is no fate or destiny, and *the three disasters* and *the eight hardships*[32] also do not exist. The Buddha's Dharma is truly refreshing and freeing.

There is no such thing as fate or destiny. Everything depends upon how you use your mind. When you are not free from attachments, those will end up becoming the causes of what you experience. Thus, ultimately, happiness and unhappiness depend upon how you use your mind.

When an actor is given a role, the actor follows the script he is given. Likewise, we are actors whose lines have been written by the effects of our own actions. And no matter whether you like your lines or not, you're not allowed to deviate from them. You are the one who made this script, this mountain of habits called fate and destiny, so you are also the one who has to melt them down.

When you were born with your body, you were already carrying with you the good and bad karma that you have accumulated over billions of eons. When this manifests, people mistakenly attribute it to fate or destiny. However, if you take everything that arises from both inside and outside of your body and entrust all of this to your foundation and let it melt down, then as "I" disappears, your old karma expires and you stop creating new karma. People who know this principle do not talk about fate and destiny.

BELIEVING IN OUTER POWERS

When problems occur, most people search for solutions from somewhere outside of themselves, instead of looking within. They rely on doctors and hospitals for problems with their body, and they try to solve their poverty by depending upon the help of others. They ask about their destiny from fortune-tellers, and they rely upon schools for education. These can be temporary solutions, but they cannot be permanent solutions. Although it is said that clothes are wings,[33] even if you wear very nice clothes, those clothes cannot become your body. Likewise, although something seems helpful, if you find it anywhere other than inside yourself, it is not a true solution. Thus it is said that above all else, you must find yourself. The wisdom and energy to take care of everything that confronts you is already within you. If you wander around looking for something outside yourself, you cannot take advantage of the unlimited solutions that are inside. Happiness does not come from something outside of us, it exists within.

If you are praying for help from some outer power, then you have already fallen into duality. No matter how much effort you spend praying like this, it cannot result in any virtue and merit. This is because everything that confronts you has arisen from your foundation, so only your foundation can take care of it.

You plant, harvest, cook, and eat your own rice. Nobody can give it to you, and nobody can do it for you. Therefore you must concentrate on developing your mind. If instead you wander around carrying an empty cup and begging for help, you will never be satisfied. Do not betray your Juingong, which has brought you here over hundreds of millions of kalpas.

If you are someone who blindly believes in outer powers, then it can be said that you have turned your back on the great and unlimited potential of a human being, the capacity to become a Buddha. If you are a human being, then as the most advanced animal, you must know to reflect upon yourself.

RELIGIOUS CONFLICT

Religion is a name. It is a name made by people according to their circumstances and geographical location, but fundamentally they are still one family. Religion ought not be something to fight over. People fight because they want to fight. God does not tell them to fight, and Jesus does not tell them to fight. Buddha does not order them to fight, and Allah does not command them to fight. People just look for an excuse to fight, so they say that they are fighting in the name of their supreme being.

Everyone's thoughts are different, but how can the truth be different? Even within Buddhism, different people believe in different ways. From some perspectives, it can even be said that they believe in different religions. If people know that the truth is one, then even though their religions have different names it is as though they all believe in the same religion. Don't say that a particular religion is the only way. Instead, if you correctly understand the teachings of your religion and put them into practice, you become humble. You will realize that you and I, you and the world, you and the universe, and you and every single thing, are one. When we are standing in front of the truth, arguments about your religion and my religion are as trivial as dust particles.

GLOSSARY

Avalokiteshvara. The Bodhisattva of compassion who hears and responds to the cries of the world, and delivers unenlightened beings from suffering.

Bhikshuni (比丘尼). Female sunims who are fully ordained are called Bhikshuni (比丘尼) sunims, while male sunims who are fully ordained are called Bhikshu (比丘) sunims. This can also be a polite way of indicating male or female sunims.

Circling a pagoda. This is a traditional devotional practice of showing reverence toward a particular pagoda or stupa and the teacher and teaching it represents.

Cultivating mind. This term includes learning how mind works, applying that knowledge, experimenting with it, and gaining experiences in order to become a free person. Studying mind, polishing mind, and practicing mind are all similar expressions.

Daean (大安), (c. 650). He was called "Daean" (Great Peace) because he sometimes went through villages shouting "Dae-an! Dae-an!" He was a recluse about whom almost nothing is known, other than that Wonhyo practiced under him after his initial enlightenment experience.

Dangun (檀君). Although Dangun (circa 2500 B.C.E.) appears in highly symbolic myths about the start of Korean civilization, he is also believed to have been a historical person. He appears to have been an awakened being who taught people on the Korean peninsula the path of spiritual awakening as well as techniques of material development.

Defilements (煩惱, klesa). This term refers to all the properties that dull the mind and are the basis for the unwholesome actions and thoughts that keep people in ignorance.

The eight hardships. These are hunger, thirst, cold, heat, water, fire, war, and disease.

The five subtle powers (五神通). 1) The ability to hear anything at any place, 2) The ability to see anything at any place, 3) The ability to know others' and feelings, 4) The ability to know past, present, and future lives, and 5) The ability to appear anywhere without moving your body.

Great questioning. This is deep, fundamental questioning that arises from within. It is sometimes translated as "Great doubt."

gwan (觀). The Korean word "gwan" literally means "watching," but in terms of spiritual practice it also means mindfulness, observing, and being aware. Gwan also includes the idea of letting go, because as you watch you allow things to flow naturally, without clinging to what has gone and without anticipating what will come.

Haengja (haeng-ja). This is someone who has entered a temple and wants to become a sunim, but who has yet to take formal vows. This is considered a training period usually lasting between one and three years, during which the haengja can see if he or she really wants to become a sunim. It also gives the temple a chance to evaluate the prospective sunim.

Hanmaum [han-ma-um]. "Han" means one, great, and combined, while "maum" means mind, as well as heart, and also means the universal consciousness that is the same in every thing and every place. Thus "Hanmaum" means both the state in which everything is interconnected as one, and also the functioning whereby everything lives and works together as a whole.

Huike (慧可). Huike was the second patriarch of Chan in China, and was the disciple of the first patriarch, Bodhidharma.

Hwadu (話頭, Chin. hua-tou, Jap. koan). Traditionally, the key phrase of an episode from the life of an ancient master, which was used for awakening practitioners, and which could not be understood intellectually. This developed into a formal training system using several hundred of the traditional 1,700 koans. However, hwadus are also fundamental questions arising from inside that we have to resolve. It has been said that your life itself is the very first hwadu that you must solve.

Juingong (主人空, ju-in-gong). Daehaeng Sunim has described Juingong as the fundamental mind with which each one of us is inherently endowed and which is directly connected to every single thing. "Juin (主人)" means the true doer, and "gong (空)" means empty. Thus Juingong (主人空) is our true nature, our true essence, which is always changing and manifesting, and which has no fixed form or shape.

karmic affinity (因緣). The connection or attraction between people or things, due to previous karmic relationships.

The main Buddha. This usually refers to the central Buddha statue on an altar, but it can also mean our own inherent Buddha.

Mani-jewels (如意珠). The round, pearl-like jewels that dragons possess, which are said to be able to grant every wish and to drive away evil. They are often used to portray the brightness and inherent ability of our fundamental mind.

Mind (心, Kor. maum). In this context, mind does not refer to the brain or intellect. This mind is intangible, invisible, beyond space and time, and has no beginning or end. It is the source of everything and everyone is endowed with it.

Samadhi (三昧). This term has been defined many ways, but it is often described as a non-dualistic state of consciousness in which it is truly understood that subject and object are not separate.

Samini (沙彌尼, sramaneri). This is the first level of ordination for a female sunim. Full ordination usually takes place after at least four more years of practice.

Samsara. This is usually thought of as the endless cycle of birth and death that all living things are continuously passing through.

Sangha. Traditionally this refers to ordained monks and nuns, but it can also mean the entire community of Buddhist believers.

Seon (禪). Chinese Chan, Japanese Zen.

Sunim. The respectful title of address for a Buddhist monk or nun in Korea. *Kun Sunim* is the polite way of addressing a very senior sunim and also can refer to a sunim considered awakened or outstanding in some other aspect of practice or study.

The three disasters. These are flood, fire, and wind.

The three realms. The upper realm, which is the realm of more advanced beings; the middle realm, which is the realm of human beings; and the lower realm, which is the realm of less developed beings and the hell realms.

Virtue and merit (功德). Here this term refers to the results of helping people or beings unconditionally and non-dually, without any thought of self or other. It becomes virtue and merit when you "do without doing," that is, doing something without the thought that "I did such and such." Because it is done unconditionally, all beings benefit from it.

Wonhyo (元曉), (617–686). Considered one of the greatest monks of Korea. He was an outstanding sunim who was known for the depth of his enlightenment and the commentaries that he wrote about various sutras, as well as for his unconventional behavior. One famous story about him says that he spent a night in a cave, and being very thirsty during the night, found some water in a broken jar. In the morning, he became sick when he saw that he had actually drunk from a broken skull and became violently ill. However, at the moment of vomiting, he realized enlightenment.

A NOTE ABOUT THE CURRENT TEXT

The contents of this book are adapted from pages 294–689 of the Korean-language book *Hanmaum Yojeon* (The Principles of Hanmaum). *Hanmaum Yojeon* was organized and edited into categories with the text coming from Dharma talks by Seon Master Daehaeng. It was designed to provide a collection of Seon Master Daehaeng's teachings organized by topic, which could be read from beginning to end, or topic by topic. *No River to Cross* follows the same general format, but some of the topics have been combined and the number of paragraphs in each section has been reduced.

Selections from *Hanmaum Yojeon* were previously published in English as *The Inner Path of Freedom*. Some of those same materials were incorporated in *No River to Cross*, but these have been carefully retranslated, and almost half of the current book is entirely newly translated text.

We would also like to express our deep gratitude to Professor Robert Buswell of UCLA, who generously agreed to write the foreword for this book.

May all beings benefit from these teachings.

With palms together,

Hanmaum International Culture Institute

September 2550 (2006 C.E.)

NOTES

1. *Sunim* is the respectful title of address for a Buddhist monk or nun in Korea. *Kun Sunim* is the polite way of addressing a very senior sunim and also can refer to a sunim considered awakened or outstanding in some other aspect of practice or study.
2. *Seon*: Chinese—Ch'an, Japanese—Zen
3. *haengja* [haeng-ja]: This is someone who has entered a temple and wants to become a sunim, but who has yet to take formal vows. This is considered a training period usually lasting between one and three years, during which the haengja can see if he or she really wants to become a sunim. It also gives the temple a chance to evaluate the prospective sunim.
4. *Bhikshuni*: Female sunims who are fully ordained are called Bhikshuni sunims, while male sunims who are fully ordained are called Bhikshu sunims.
5. This is the first level of ordination for a female sunim (sramaneri).
6. *Juingong* [ju-in-gong]: Daehaeng Sunim has described Juingong as the fundamental mind with which each one of us is inherently endowed and which is directly connected to every single thing. "Juin" means the true doer, and "gong" means empty. Thus Juingong is our true nature, our true essence, which is always changing and manifesting, and which has no fixed form or shape.
7. *Mani-jewels* are round, pearl-like jewels that dragons possess, which are said to be able to grant every wish and to drive away evil. They are often used to portray the brightness and inherent ability of our fundamental mind.
8. This is an ancient symbol in Buddhist countries that represents the all-pervading and unhindered functioning of the truth.
9 *Hanmaum* [han-ma-um]: "Han" means one, great, and combined, while "maum" means mind, as well as heart, and also means the

universal consciousness that is the same in every thing and every place. Thus "Hanmaum" means both the state in which everything is inter-connected as one, and also the functioning whereby everything lives and works together as a whole.

10. *mind*: [Kor.—maum] Mind, in this text, does not refer to the brain or intellect. This mind is intangible, invisible, beyond space and time, and has no beginning or end. It is the source of everything and everyone is endowed with it.

11. *The three realms*: The upper realm, which is the realm of more advanced beings; the middle realm, which is the realm of human beings; and the lower realm, which is the realm of less developed beings and the hell beings.

12. *Virtue and merit* here means helping people or beings unconditionally and non-dually, without any thought of self or other. It becomes virtue and merit when you "do without doing," that is, doing something without the thought that "I did such and such." Because it is done uncondi-tionally, all beings benefit from it.

13. *The main Buddha*: This usually refers to the central Buddha statue on an altar, but it can also mean our own inherent Buddha.

14. *karmic affinity*: This is similar to karma, but it refers to the connection or attraction between people or things, due to previous karmic relationships.

15. *Samsara*: This is usually thought of as the endless cycle of birth and death that all living things are continuously passing through.

16. *The four types of lives* are lives born from eggs, born from the womb, born from moisture, and born through transformation.

17. *Circling a pagoda* is a traditional devotional practice of showing rever-ence toward a particular pagoda or stupa and the teacher and teaching it represents.

18. Although Dangun (circa 2500 B.C.E.) appears in highly symbolic myths about the start of Korean civilization, he is also believed to have been a historical person. He appears to have been an awakened being who taught people on the Korean peninsula the path of spiritual awakening as well as techniques of material development.

19. *Cultivating mind* includes learning how mind works, applying that knowledge, experimenting with it, and gaining experiences in order to become a free person. Studying mind, polishing mind, and practicing mind are all similar expressions.

20. Daehaeng Sunim has often warned people about this stage, saying that it is easy for people to deceive themselves about their own progress.

She teaches people that they must continuously die to what they have experienced and what they think they know. Even though it is something from your fundamental mind, you have to let go of that again to your foundation. You shouldn't just follow what comes out. It often happens that people are deceived by the things that arise from their karmic consciousness or from their own likes and dislikes, mistaking those for something from their fundamental mind. Everything has to be returned to your foundation. You have to let go of things that are unpleasant as well as things that seem wonderful again and again in order to grow and develop in your practice.

She often says, "You have to continue to practice diligently so that 'I' cannot find a foothold in your life." Once we start holding on to what we have experienced or what we think we know, then even the things from our foundation can become hindrances. They become footholds for our likes and dislikes, for our discriminating intellect, and for the karmic consciousnesses within our body.

About these karmic consciousnesses, Daehaeng Sunim has said, "These return to you as you have input them, but because people often experience these through their consciousness, they think that those thoughts and feelings are 'me,' and so are deceived by them. It's as if they are trying to take revenge upon you." The way to handle these karmic consciousnesses is to let go again and again, to continuously entrust to your foundation whatever comes from inside or outside.

We can check our practice by being aware of things that are the opposite of spiritual development. These are states of mind or behaviors that are not in harmony with the fundamental truths of this world, and so hinder our development and lead only to suffering. There are several states of mind that warn us we've gone astray, such as blaming and criticizing others, stubbornness, resisting change, arguing about right and wrong, and having an unkind or harsh frame of mind.

21. *Avalokiteshvara Bodhisattva* is the Bodhisattva of Compassion who hears and responds to the cries of the world, and delivers unenlightened beings from suffering.

22. *Gwan*: The Korean word "gwan" literally means "watching," but in terms of spiritual practice it also means mindfulness, observing, and being aware. Gwan also includes the idea of letting go, because as you watch you allow things to flow naturally, without clinging to what has gone and without anticipating what will come.

23. *Defilements* (klesa) refers to all the properties that dull the mind and are the basis for the unwholesome actions and thoughts that keep people in ignorance.

24. This is sometimes translated as "Great doubt."

25. *Hwadu* (Chin.—hua-tou, Jap.—koan): Traditionally, the key phrase of an episode from the life of an ancient master, which was used for awakening practitioners, and which could not be understood intellectually. This developed into a formal training system using several hundred of the traditional 1,700 koans. However hwadus are also fundamental questions arising from inside that we have to resolve. It has been said that your life itself is the fundamental hwadu that you must first solve.

26. *Samadhi* has been defined many ways, but it is often described as a non-dualistic state of consciousness in which it is truly understood that subject and object are not separate.

27. *The five subtle powers* are the ability to hear anything at any place, the ability to see anything at any place, the ability to know others' thoughts and feelings, the ability to know past, present, and future lives, and the ability to appear anywhere without moving your body.

28. Sangha traditionally refers to ordained monks and nuns, but it can also mean the entire community of Buddhist believers.

29. *Wonhyo* (617–686): Considered one of the greatest monks of Korea. He was an outstanding sunim who was known for the depth of his enlightenment and the commentaries that he wrote about various sutras, as well as for his unconventional behavior. One famous story about him says that he spent a night in a cave, and being very thirsty during the night, found some water in a broken jar. In the morning, he saw that he had actually drunk from a broken skull and became violently ill. However, at the moment of vomiting, he realized enlightenment.

30. *Daean* (dates unknown): He was called "Daean" (Great Peace) because he sometimes went through villages shouting "Dae-an! Dae-an!" He was a recluse about whom almost nothing is known, other than that Wonhyo practiced under him after his initial enlightenment experience.

31. *Huike*: He was the second patriarch of Chan in China, and was the disciple of the first patriarch, Bodhidharma.

32. The three disasters are flood, fire, and wind. The eight hardships are hunger, thirst, cold, heat, water, fire, war, and disease.

33. This is a Korean expression meaning roughly that a nice appearance can create all kinds of opportunities.

ABOUT WISDOM PUBLICATIONS

Wisdom Publications, a nonprofit publisher, is dedicated to making available authentic works relating to Buddhism for the benefit of all. We publish books by ancient and modern masters in all traditions of Buddhism, translations of important texts, and original scholarship. Additionally, we offer books that explore East-West themes unfolding as traditional Buddhism encounters our modern culture in all its aspects. Our titles are published with the appreciation of Buddhism as a living philosophy, and with the special commitment to preserve and transmit important works from Buddhism's many traditions.

To learn more about Wisdom, or to browse books online, visit our website at www.wisdompubs.org.

You may request a copy of our catalog online or by writing to this address:

Wisdom Publications
199 Elm Street
Somerville, Massachusetts 02144 USA
Telephone: 617-776-7416
Fax: 617-776-7841
Email: info@wisdompubs.org
www.wisdompubs.org

THE WISDOM TRUST

As a nonprofit publisher, Wisdom is dedicated to the publication of Dharma books for the benefit of all sentient beings and dependent upon the kindness and generosity of sponsors in order to do so. If you would like to make a donation to Wisdom, you may do so through our website or our Somerville office. If you would like to help sponsor the publication of a book, please write or email us at the address above.

Thank you.

Wisdom is a nonprofit, charitable 501(c)(3) organization affiliated with the Foundation for the Preservation of the Mahayana Tradition (FPMT).

Polishing the Diamond, Enlightening the Mind
Reflections of a Korean Buddhist Master
Jae Woong Kim * Foreword by His Holiness the Dalai Lama
272 pages, ISBN 0-86171-145-9, $18.95

"A remarkable book. Kim has written a series of detailed and emotional personal stories, vivid and quirky anecdotes, and elegant Buddhist lessons. Though the practice of Buddhism is thousands of years old, Kim's voice and his reflections are both modern and timeless, dealing with universal and never-ending challenges. Kim's book, through the Diamond Sutra's teachings and experiences of his own life, shows us ways to cultivate our minds and end our cycles of greed, self-serving behaviors, wrong decisions, and many lifetimes of suffering... A wonderful addition to anyone's library, regardless of their relationship to Buddhism or Korea."—*Korean Quarterly*

Everything Yearned For
Manhae's Poems of Love and Longing
Translated and introduced by Francisca Cho
144 pages, 6.45 x 7.5, hardcover, ISBN 0-86171-489-X, $15.00

"It's cause for celebration when one book can brighten so much darkness. Francisca Cho's definitive translation of Manhae's *The Silence of Everything Yearned For* is a revelatory experience, a wonderful journey to the heart of the heart, gently and wisely guided by a true master. This is the only book-length collection of poems ever published by Manhae (the pen name of the revered Korean activist-monk-poet Han Yong-un). Manhae not only bore witness to the history of his time but also took a leading part in it... Cho's indispensable English-language rendition also includes several chapters of skillful commentary on the poems' interwoven topics of Buddhism, activism, and love. In its mode of variations on a central theme— that of love—*Everything Yearned For* speaks to us more deeply than any linear narrative might. Rilke's *Sonnets to Orpheus* comes quickly to mind, as do Whitman's original *Leaves of Grass* and Tagore's *Lover's Gift.*"—*Tricycle*

Contents

The Property Investors Management Handbook

Introduction